FAITH ALIVE!

John and
Barbara Brokhoff

FAITH ALIVE!

ISBN 0-89536-342-9   PRINTED IN U.S.A.

*This book is dedicated
with love and appreciation
to the churches we served in
Georgia
Missouri
North Carolina
Pennsylvania
Virginia
— John and Barbara Brokhoff*

TABLE OF CONTENTS

The Christian's Happy Hour

The Thirteenth Sunday After Pentecost

Barbara Brokhoff

Addressing one another in psalms and hymns and spiritual songs, singing and making melody to the Lord with all your heart . . . [Ephesians 5:19]

A radio commercial recently advertised a place in Atlanta called "Anthony's" whose Happy Day on Saturdays begins at 11:30 A.M. Most places that sell alcoholic beverages have happy hour from 4 to 7 P.M. Happy Hour for the Christian should be the hour of worship on Sunday morning, but how do you *honestly* feel when you are awakened by the alarm on the Lord's Day and you realize it is another "Church Day"? Can you hardly wait for the service time to roll around, or do you roll over in bed, moan and groan and cover your head, and wish that once, just this once, you could sleep in and forget the whole thing? Is the thought of worship agony or ecstasy? Do you overflow with delight just to think about it? Is it "Happy Hour" for you?

Today's text makes us think of the singing in our worship. Is the singing in our church something that brings special blessing and joy to you, or are the hymns sung with blasphemous dullness, apathy, lethargy, indifference, and drudgery?

America's music has come from everywhere: We have mountain music, music out of the West, songs of the South. We've had ballads and blues and Rock 'n' Roll. Then there are waltzes, jazz, spirituals, gospel songs. And then the appearance of singing radio commercials and finally television commercials that laud Hamm's Beer from "the land of sky-blue waters," Pepsi-Cola for those who "think young," and

McDonald's Hamburgers because "you deserve a break today."

But the people of God sing "hit" tunes too. Everyone has a favorite, but nationally "The Old Rugged Cross," "Rock of Ages," "Blessed Assurance," "I Love To Tell the Story," and "How Great Thou Art" perennially stay in the top running. Some of our hits are the great hymns, the gospel songs, the anthems, and the Psalms — depending on who we are, where we grew up, and what we sang as a child.

The text tells us all about the whom and the why and the how and the what of singing:

Sing to the Lord!

"Making melody to the Lord . . ."

We sing to almost everything else under the sun these days, rather than to God. We sing to animals, to the moon, to the stars, to our children, to each other; we sing to the waterfowl, a blind bat, or more recently there was a "Ballad to a Bread Wrapper!"

But who sings to *God* in our time? Or are you *supposed* to enjoy your faith? Does your religion make your heart lighten with an almost uncontrollable need to express it in music and song — or is the service something to be *endured* until it's over one more time and you can get to your favorite cafeteria to enjoy a good Sunday dinner?

The Psalms literally resound with the music of a worshiper who can hardly wait to get to church. He said, "O come, let us sing unto the Lord: let us make a joyful noise to the rock of our salvation. Let us come before His Presence with thanksgiving." The translation of "let us come before His Presence" is — *"Let us hurry up and come into his presence."* Can't you just see him pacing the floor, anxious, excited, clock-watching, impatient? We can't wait for the happy hour of worship to start!

We ought to come to church breathless, not because we are late again, but because we are so eager for the praise to the Lord to begin.

Think! We are coming to meet God — not just anybody, but God! Shouldn't the delightful suspense make our breath short, and our hearts beat faster? When my husband, John, is due home, and then finally I hear his car drive into the driveway, the car door slams shut, and soon his step on the front porch, I feel a racing pulse and a great anticipation because *my John* is home again!

Should a mere mortal man set our pulses throbbing more than the presence of an omnipotent, transcendent, and immanent God?

Faith that is real, vibrant, earnest, and alive needs *proclaiming* — and singing gives us opportunity to exult in him, to adore him, and to thank him.

Why Sing to the Lord?

"Addressing one another in psalms and hymns and spiritual songs, singing . . ."

Why should we *sing* our praises to the Lord, why not just *say* them? Because words are the expression of the head, but music is the expression of the heart — so in singing we put head and heart together to praise God.

It's true that just reading the words of the hymns helps you. A great way to prepare yourself for the happy hour of worship after you arrive at church is to read the hymns before the hour begins — while the organist or pianist is playing the prelude you can pray and praise by reading the words in the hymnal. (It's a lot better practice than assessing the number of people at worship, the clothes that each is wearing, the hair-do of the woman in front of you, or carrying on a conversation with your neighbor).

But *singing* still is better than *reading* the hymn! It

affects you more than you realize. It changes you, your attitude, and your spirit. Singing locates your senses on God, not self. You may sometimes not *feel* like singing — then sing away — offer, as Paul says, "a sacrifice of praise to God."

There are times when we do feel badly, discouraged, despairing, and our hearts are heavy — tears roll down our cheeks and singing is difficult — but the Old Testament prophet says "God giveth songs in the night."

Everyone needs to participate in the singing at Happy Hour. Even if you don't sing well, even if you can't "carry a tune in a bucket," even if you don't have a good voice — God is not looking for professional singers at the service. He is listening for the music of a heart that loves him and refuses to keep quiet about it.

How Sing?

". . . with all your heart."

Practice and experience have taught us that some ways to sing are better than others. The singing should not be so fast that you can't catch the meaning of the message, but the sin against singing that we usually commit is the opposite; we sing with such blasphemous slowness. God must be embarrased and offended when we drag to its death a bright hymn like "Joyful, Joyful, We Adore Thee" or sing "All Hail the Power of Jesus Name" as if we were attending a wake or funeral.

We must sing lustily, not as if we were half dead or half asleep, but lift our voices with strength and confidence. How good it is to hear a Christian "belt out" the hymns with fervor and earnestness!

Wesley told his followers to sing spiritually — to "have an eye on God with every word you sing — aim at pleasing him, not yourself or others."

We absolutely must learn to sing thoughtfully. Carefully note the meaning of the words you sing. It is easy to pay so little attention to the message of a song that we often sing what we do not mean. Did you ever notice the commitments and promises we make in the tunes we sing? Some things we sing to music we would never say without the impulse of the melody.

How about: "Take my silver and my gold, not a mite would I withhold?" Do you mean *that*?

Or: "O for a thousand tongues to sing my great Redeemer's praise." What would you do with a *thousand* tongues when *one* does not even do its best in witness for him?

Or: "Have Thine own way, Lord, hold o'er my being *absolute* sway." Now that's a *big* request of total commitment — are you ready for that?

And do you *understand* what you sing: "Come Thou Fount of Every Blessing — Here I raise my Ebenezer"? What does "Ebenezer" mean? What are you raising to God?

Let us sing the words with all our heart, may our lips frame the words, but may our inner being affirm it with all of ourselves!

What to Sing?

"Addressing one another in psalms and hymns and spiritual songs,"

The Hebrew Hymnal was the Psalms. It must have been a Psalm that Paul and Silas were singing at midnight in the jail at Philippi when God heard them and sent his earthquake angel to keep time with the music and to open the doors of the prison.

Something terrible has happened to the Psalms in our time. The modern mind has lost them, one after another, till now we are down to one or two: the 23rd Psalm or maybe Old Hundreth or the 121st Psalm.

Did you realize our early fathers knew all the Psalms

almost as well as Jesus did? Christians, condemned to
die, entered the Roman arenas singing: "I will bless the
Lord at all times." It is said that Thomas More waited for
his execution with some lines from Psalm 51. John Huss
stepped up to his stake in 1415 reciting Psalm 31. Martin
Luther's famous hymn "A Mighty Fortress Is Our God"
was born out of Psalm 46. Methodists like to remember
that John Wesley died with the words of that same
Psalm on his lips.

History tells us that St. Benedict told all the monks in
his monastery to sing the words of the 95th Psalm in
unison the first thing upon arising. What Psalm do *you*
sing when you get out of bed — or could you call it a
Psalm — or could you even call it singing?

And hymns can be so appropriate to our worship. In
the proper place in a worship service the hymn makes it
possible for us to respond to what God is offering us. A
great hymn of praise and adoration prepares our hearts
for God to speak. Suppose you want to pray, but you
can't think how to frame the words? — Find a prayer
hymn and make its message your own. Some of the best
prayers we ever utter are joined with words and music
that express the depths of our hearts.

And sometimes we sing a hymn or song simply
because of the association. It may not even be
necessarily appropriate, perhaps there is no real reason
nor logic for liking it — but maybe you learned it as a
child, or your mother sang it, or your father said it was
his favorite, or it was sung at a loved one's funeral — any
number of sentimental reasons — but the result is that
you *like* the song and *love* to sing it!

Then sing it and enjoy it and worship with it!

My dying mother sang three songs a few hours before
she died. They were "Whispering Hope," "Rock of
Ages," and "The Sweet By and By." It is true that the
"Sweet By and By" does not have the same quality of
theology as some of Wesley's or Luther's hymns, but
because *my* mother sang it, I will always love it. It says

something to me still these twenty years later to recall her voice saying:

> *There's a land that is fairer than day,*
> *And by faith we can see it afar;*
> *For the Father waits over the way,*
> *To prepare us a dwelling place there.*
> *In the sweet by and by,*
> *We shall meet on that beautiful shore.*

The secular Happy Hour is a place of conversation, conviviality, and cordial fellowship. The Christian Happy Hour should be no less — so be filled with the Spirit and let your hour with God be merry with mirth and music!

14

Boss, Buddy, or Both?

The Fourteenth Sunday After Pentecost

A dialogue sermon by John and Barbara Brokhoff

Wives, be subject to your husbands, as to the Lord. [Ephesians 5:22]

Husbands, love your wives, as Christ loved the church and gave himself up for her. [Ephesians 5:25]

John: Barbara, what is the first thing you read in the paper?

Barbara: I read the headlines, Ann Landers, and Peanuts. What is the first thing you read, John?

J: I read the headlines, Ann Landers, and the Street Scenes in the Atlanta *Journal.* Do you remember the one that told of a service station attendant, washing the "Just Married" markings off a car, saying to the bride and groom, "So you've been married just forty-five minutes. I've been married three years, the awfullest three years of my life!"

B: I remember reading it and thinking how sad it was. Why do you suppose there are so many people who think that marriage must mean unhappiness and trouble?

J: There are a multitude of reasons, of course, but one possible reason why they can't get along with each other is that they can't decide who is boss. Or do you think there needs to be a boss in marriage? You're a woman. How do you feel about this? Remember that in marriage two people are coming into one union. The two parts become one while each part remains intact — you don't just melt in each other. Each person remains a separate entity but must still work closely with the other. Like two pistons running closely together in an engine — how can it be done without friction?

B: Marriage motors need STP the same as automobile engines. Ways must be found to help the relationship run smoothly — and to answer your other question: Yes, I do feel that a family needs a boss. Every group or organization that works seems to need a head, a leader, a "boss," if you want to call it that. Business needs a boss, clubs need a president or leader, athletic teams need a head, the church needs a head pastor to guide, and so on. Therefore it seems that marriage will need a leader as well. Somebody needs to be the spokesman, the leader, the one who makes the final decision in the event of an impasse — but *who* is to be the boss in marriage?

J: You probably read, as I did, that the U.S. Census Bureau has decided in 1980 to delete the question: "Head of the household?" from its questionnaire. They have so many problems with the answer, so many arguments resulting from it, they are leaving it out. But if a marriage *needs* a head, do you feel the wife should be the boss?

B: You may find this answer strange, John, but no, generally, I'd have to say it should not be the wife. There are exceptions to this, of course, but I feel this role leads to unhappy husbands, to the fear of domination, and frankly, I don't think it is the biblical ideal or standard. Don't you tell a story about men dominated by women?

J: Yes, remember, there was a long line of men standing in front of the Pearly Gates, waiting to be admitted to heaven. A sign overhead read: FOR MEN WHO

16

HAVE BEEN DOMINATED ALL THEIR LIVES BY THEIR WIVES. The line was long, extending as far as the eye could see. Then there was another sign nearby which read: FOR MEN WHO HAVE NEVER BEEN DOMINATED BY THEIR WIVES. One lone man was standing under this sign. St. Peter came over to him and said, "What are you standing here for?" The man replied, "I don't know. My wife told me to stand here!"

B: Lots of marriages are dominated by wives, but sometimes it is a child or the children who seem to be boss. It is surprising how many households are ruled by the desire and whim of the offspring. This is not good for the marriage or the child. But, John, I feel that the Bible speaks to the real answer in the text before us. In Ephesians 5:22 it says: "Wives, be subject to your husbands, as to the Lord." Doesn't that say clearly who is to be the leader in the home? But I must hasten to add that it certainly doesn't mean the husband is to be a despot, a tyrant, or a dictator. Cruelty is *out*! Wife-beating is a major social problem. The Atlanta *Journal* reported that in Boston police receive forty-five wife-beating reports a day. Sixty percent of the police calls at night in Atlanta are for domestic disturbances, many of them wife-beating cases. One out of eight of the 19,500 murders in the nation in 1975 involved a spouse killing a spouse, according to the FBI. "It's a hidden problem," says Allan Rogers, director of the Massachusetts Law Reform Institute. "Many people don't consider this a serious thing. They say 'every man has the right to beat his wife once in a while.' " — Now, John, *that* is not what the Bible has in mind when it gives leadership to the husband!

J: Certainly not, the husband must always remember that he is subject first of all to Christ, and without being truly Christian he can never exercise properly his responsibility of leadership. But do you feel this makes a woman feel inferior, unequal, and shoddy?

B: No, because I am *not* inferior to a man. I feel that God made us equals, but he did give us different roles and functions to fill. I said last night, or sometime, that Christianity doesn't discriminate between sexes anymore than between races — but it does *differentiate*! Because I am submissive to you does not debilitate me in any way. But I warn you, not everyone feels this way. In practice, don't you think the traditional role of the husband has changed today?

J: Yes, often both husband and wife work outside the home. The husband does as many household chores as does the wife. He helps with the cooking, diapers the baby, does the laundry and cleaning. This is both good and bad. Certainly there is nothing wrong with his carrying an equal share of the task. But it does sometimes mean that the lines of leadership become fuzzy, he and she are uncertain of their roles, and then again a husband may simply default his role of responsible leadership. It is easier for him if the wife does it. It is simpler, less complicated, leaves him more time for other things. Consequently respect and authority of the man erodes and ultimately is lost.

B: John, the other half of this text in Ephesians helps us to see the role of the husband and wife another way. In verse 22 of chapter 5 the wife is subject to the man; in verse 25 the man is shown he must love his wife — love her as much as Christ loved the church, and that was enough to die for it! In fact, that's one really good reason why I find it so easy to submit to you. I know you love me enough to die for me, I know you love me far more than you love yourself, so submission in that relationship is all joy! And that takes away a lot of the problem of "Boss" — because in reality we have become "Buddies." Love makes us buddies, friends, companions, and lovers.

J: Do you remember the story of the small boys who were going to Scout camp for the first time? Before the time for swimming began, the leader explained the buddy system. Each boy was to have a buddy whom he kept his eye on at all times. When the scoutmaster blew the whistle each was to find his buddy and hold up his hand high. "Now," said the leader, "What is a buddy?" "A buddy is someone who drowns with you," said one small tenderfoot. — Now, Barbara, that's really what it is in marriage too. A buddy is the other half of the equal team. As you need two on a bicycle built for two, like two blades on scissors — both necessary for it to work.

B: Yes, and buddies always comfort and help you in difficult situations. I read an excellent example of this in this story: It seems that a wife and husband were in flight on a long-planned vacation trip. Suddenly she was horror-struck by a burst of memory. "O my!" she said, "I just remembered I forgot to turn off the iron!" Her husband was not upset at all, but very composed. "Don't worry, honey," he said, "Nothing in our house can burn for long. I forgot to turn off the water in the bathtub." Now that's a real buddy for you, isn't it, John?

J: We need to become real buddies. We need to stay in one world, learn to grow together, not apart. Do you remember the photographer who attended one of our revivals and said that the hardest pictures he had to take were those of couples who were celebrating twenty-fifth or thirtieth anniveraries? We asked him why and he said he had trouble getting them to *touch* each other. Isn't that sad?

B: It reminds me of the woman who wrote to the newspaper columnist asking for advice. She said: "My husband, when we first married, used to like to 'cuddle' in bed, now when I move close to him he accuses me of 'leaning on him' — shall we get twin beds?" That's not becoming buddies, either, is it?

J: One of the real problems of marriage is keeping the lines of communication open. Buddies, you know, share many things: secrets, desires, goals, dreams. Many couples are unable to communicate. Some subjects are completely taboo. Some never discuss religion, or maybe politics, or it might be sex, or money, or the in-laws, property. It is extremely detrimental to a relationship when large areas are "off-limits" for discussion and communication. I love the way we discuss everything —

B: So do I, even if you are boss, and even have your mind already made up, you at least let me *talk* about it! (And if my logic is good enough you may even change your mind!)

J: And it pleases me that each time I come home from teaching at the seminary you never fail to ask me how my classes have gone, how was my day, do I feel well, and did I take my medicine —

B: You are even better than I. In fact I'm barely in the door each evening when I return from revival services but you ask me about the meeting, the sermon, and so on.

J: You grow together, not only by communicating, but also by knowing each other thoroughly. In the best-selling book *Passages* the author states that husbands who are asked to describe their run-away wives are often unable to do so. When asked what color are her eyes they will usually say "blue"; hair, they will respond "dishwater blonde"; habits (they leave this one blank); and for characteristics they will write "emotional." When we don't take time to *notice* and *know* each other well, we can never build good foundations for marriage. This is true with the entire family. It would be a good plan for each family to have at least one night a week that is "family night." You might go fishing together, to a movie, play games, read a book aloud, plan a project, visit some near-by attraction — but *doing things together* makes for good buddies!

B: That's true — and buddies usually like the same things. That doesn't mean that we must become carbon copies of each other. We should never lose our individuality. You, John, will always be more reserved and dignified than I — while I am much more voluble and outgoing than you. It would be a shame for either of us to try to imitate the other and fail to be our true selves. But, it *is* good to have as many things in common as possible. Do you remember the young couple who were getting married and the only three foods they liked in common were cookies, clam chowder, and cheeseburgers? Now *that* is a lot of individuality!

J: The really important place for mutuality, however, is in the more fundamental things. It is important that we have a common outlook on life, a common purpose in life, and a meeting of the minds on the values of life.

J: Well, which will it be then: Boss or buddy? Which do you think makes for the good marriage?

B: I believe that the more of a buddy you are in marriage, the less you need a boss!

J: Love is something that continues to grow — it never remains static — it either dies or it grows.

B: Then we are going to keep love *alive by loving*!

Being Christian Without Being Religious

The Fifteenth Sunday After Pentecost

John R. Brokhoff

If one thinks he is religious, and does not bridle his tongue but deceives his heart, this man's religion is vain. Religion that is pure and undefiled before God and the Father is this: to visit orphans and widows in their affliction, and to keep oneself unstained from the world. [James 1:26, 27]

Do you think of yourself as a religious person? If you are like most Americans, you would answer affirmatively. A recent Gallup poll indicates that ninety-eight percent of Americans believe in God, seventy-three percent believe in life after death, and sixty-five percent believe even in hell. If Paul came to America as he did to Athens, he would say the same about us. As he walked in Athens, he saw a monument to every God. In fear of missing one, they even erected a monument to the unknown God. He commented, "I perceive that you are very religious." If he came to our land, he would see churches, clergy, and church members galore. He would notice that we have a god for every interest in life: a god of money, a god of self, a god of sex. You name it and we have a god for it. Indeed, we are a religious people.

We may be religious, but are we Christian? It is as easy to be religious as it is hard to be Christian. It is quite possible to be religious without being Christian, and it is also possible to be Christian without being religious. This is what our text is all about. The men of Athens were religious but were not Christian. James talks about two kinds of religion. One is vain; it is what we mean by "religious." It is an end in itself. The other is pure and true religion which we mean by Christianity.

This is a religion which is a means to an end. Thus, we are faced with the question whether we are religious or whether we are Christian.

Through this text God is showing us how we can easily be religious without being Christian. James refers to a man who thinks he is religious but does not bridle his tongue: "This man's religion is vain." He is a religious man but not a Christian.

Marks of the Religious

When are we religious and not Christian? When we hold to orthodoxy, we are religious. Orthodoxy takes the faith and freezes it into dogmatic formulations and creeds. We are sure that we have the truth once and for all time delivered to us. To defend and protect this faith we spell it out in rational statements and we demand that everyone accept these statements or they cannot be considered Christians. We exclude those who do not agree with us. We refuse to have pulpit and altar fellowship with them. In the name of orthodoxy, the church has been guilty even of murder. Repeatedly in the history of the church we find people labelled heretics and put to death for their variant beliefs. Protestants were no better than Catholics because, for instance, in the 16th century under the leadership of John Calvin, Servetus, a man who had difficulty with the Trinity, was condemned and burned to death. It was the practice in this same period to drown people who insisted upon immersion as a mode of baptism. And all of this in the name of orthodoxy!

In our time, we are really no better. There are still churches who claim that they have the only faith and they refuse to recognize others as Christians because they do not agree with creedal formulations. There are some who still claim that the water in baptism must be of a certain quantity and application before a person can be considered a Christian. On Communion Sundays you can find churches with doctrinal statements in their bulletins saying that only those who believe this very thing about Holy Communion may come to the Lord's Table. Others are absolutely sure that no one has the Holy Spirit unless he has an emotional experience and speaks in tongues. Without the ability to speak in unintelligible language, they claim you do not have the Spirit and without the Spirit you are not a born-again Christian.

Another type of being "religious" is pietism. These people go around proud of their religious performances. They love to pray and fold their hands in piety. They consider themselves wearing a halo. They love to mumble prayers and to be seen regularly at worship. They would not miss a day reading their Bibles. They are "goody-goody" people. They make a show of their religion, but it amounts to only a show. A deacon one time heard his church janitor swearing. He took the janitor to task about it and scolded him for his unchristian behavior. The janitor replied, "Yes, deacon, I do a little swearing and you do a little praying. And neither of us means anything by it." And this is the way it is with this type of religious person. The words we say, the hymns we sing, and the faith we profess just do not make any difference to us.

The pietists are long on their rituals but short on their performance of what they claim to believe. Some can get so busy in church activities that they do not have time to be Christian. One of my advisees for the Doctor of Sacred Theology degree spent a quarter in Atlanta's inner city. He was asked to serve a summons on a lady whose house was sub-standard. There was a leaking pipe that made the back yard into a quagmire. He tried a number of times to find her at home but always failed. He inquired about her and learned that she was hardly ever home because she was a busy church worker. In desperation the summons had to be mailed to her. When she received it, she became so angry that she evicted the tenants for making the complaint to the authorities. You would call her a pious woman, a religious woman. But, would you consider her a Christian?

Another form of being religious is legalism. Here the emphasis is placed upon the law of God in terms of the letter and not the spirit. Most church members can be labelled as legalists, because most of us live by the law. We have put ourselves into a straitjacket in terms of "Thou shalt not." We live by the letter of the law and we make ourselves miserable in trying to keep the law down to the dotting of the "i" and the crossing of the "t." This takes all the joy out of being a Christian and causes many of us to be nervous saints. While I was a student at the seminary, I spent a summer taking a special course in physical and mental health at Pennsylvania Hospital. A fellow-student, a Presbyterian, and I went to the Jersey shore one Sunday afternoon. We went to the beach but he would not go into the water because he felt it was a violation of the law, "Remember the sabbath day to keep it holy." His conscience would allow him to go to the beach, to sit on the sand, and to put on his swim trunks. But, he could not put his feet into the water because it was against the law in his own mind. While I was enjoying a swim, he was perfectly miserable because of his legalistic attitude toward religion.

Not only does legalism take the joy out of being a Christian, but the law can even keep us from doing what is right and good. Jesus had this problem in his day with the religious leaders who were legalists. They objected **strenuously to Jesus' helping and healing a person on the** Sabbath. Jesus chose to ignore the law as man-made and insisted that it was right to do good on the Sabbath. Thus, he healed people. He reminded the Pharisees that the sabbath was made for man and not man for the sabbath. In various instances it is quite possible to break the law of God by trying to keep the law of God, according to the letter and not the spirit of the law. This may be religious but it is not Christian.

Consider another aspect of being religious. It is institutionalism. In this case we are all for religion in terms of the church as an institution and an establishment. We are all for it as an end in itself. We have been thinking that a great church is a big church. We have measured the greatness of the church by the bigness of the preacher. We have taken much pride in our real estate, and we have developed an edifice complex. We boast of the church's size. We publicize our big budget. We tell our friends how many ranks of pipes the organ has. The stained glass windows are out of this world. The pews are the most comfortable in the state, and the church is delightfully air conditioned. In our love of the institution, we have even contorted the work of the church. Evangelism is not to bring souls from sin to a saving relationship with Christ but a means of building up the church rolls that we could brag about the size of the church. We have been intensely concerned about stewardship, but it was not in the sense of an expression of faith and love of God but we just had to have the money to run the establishment that we have built. More and more the church has become concerned about its programs for every age but in doing so we have forgotten about people and their personal, spiritual needs.

Now what does God think about all of this religion? James would say that all of it is "vain" — meaningless, worthless. Have you ever stopped to think that God could be in opposition to religion? When we say our prayers and sing our liturgy, do you think God could possibly be upset about all of this? It is possible that religion itself can be an enemy of God, because every time religion becomes an end in itself, it becomes a god opposed to God. If you want to know what God thinks about this type of religion, you need to turn to prophets like Isaiah and Amos. Speaking through Isaiah, God thundered, "When you come to appear before me, who required of you this trampling of my courts? Bring no more vain offerings; incense is an abomination to me . . . I cannot endure iniquity and solemn assembly . . . when you spread forth your hands, I will hide my eyes from you; even though you make many prayers, I will not listen . . ." Amos says in behalf of God: "I hate, I despise your feasts and I take no delight in your solemn assemblies . . . Take away from me the noise of your songs; to the melody of your harps I will not listen." If you, by chance, happen to be a religious person, don't count on it that you are pleasing God by your religious devotions and liturgical movements. A man does not go to Heaven because he is religious. That kind of religion is vain. It will do you no good. In fact, it irritates God.

Christian But Not Religious

Through this text God is also saying to us that we can be Christian without being religious. James refers to a religion that is pure and undefiled before God. What kind of religion is that? It is a religion that is not an end in itself but it is a means to an end. The text says, "Religion that is pure and undefiled before God and the Father is this . . ." "Is this." What is "this"? It is service to God and man. A Christian is one who is not only a hearer but a doer of the word. Prayer must end in performance. Worship eventuates in work. Confession of the faith must lead to expression of the faith. You must not misunderstand what we are saying here. We are not saying that to be Christian we cut ourselves off from all religious devotions. By all means, we need prayer, worship, Bible reading, and churches. Without these we would have only a banal humanitarianism. We would amount to nothing but do-gooders. The church would turn into an ethical society. What we mean to say is that to be Christian we must go beyond all of our religiosity to a practical expression of faith in the lives of people in terms of service. Accordingly, our religion is a means to an end, and not an end in itself.

How is this faith expressed? James tells us in our text that to be Christian is to have a concern for the social ills of society. He put it this way: "to visit orphans and widows in their affliction . . ." True Christianity is a deep concern about people living in affliction, in trouble, and misery. In James' day, the afflicted were the fatherless and the husbandless. Orphans and widows are not a problem for us in our time. Who are the orphans and widows of our day? They are the people of America — thirty-four million of them — caught in the trap of poverty. They are the unfortunate ones living in slum ghettos such as a family of five living in one room without refrigeration or running water. One naked light hangs from the ceiling. There is no stove, only one hotplate. One window is in the room and it looks out upon a brick wall eight inches away. There is one bathroom for the floor that must be used by eight families. Rats and roaches are partners in sharing this room with people. The afflicted of our day are the 10,000 people in the world who die daily from starvation. The "orphans" are the one million youth who annually fall into juvenile crime and get sent away to reform schools to become hardened criminals. They are the tens of thousands of youth who are addicted to drugs and cannot get free. They are the millions in America who are victims of racial, economic, and political discrimination.

What can we do about these people living in affliction? If we are Christian, we will do all within our power and resources to help them. The most that we can do is to give these people our concern and love. More than money these people need love, sweet love. In Wilkerson's *Cross and Switchblade*, he asked a gang leader what is the main problem among the ghetto youth of that area. The answer was "loneliness." Imagine loneliness as the main problem in the midst of eight million people! Yet it is the truth, because this loneliness comes from a sense of not having anyone to care. Most of us do not realize that almost every person today is lonely and burdened with problems. They are hurting and crying out for someone to listen to them, to care about them. It is reported that one of our greatest needs is for counseling. Physicians, psychiatrists, and pastors have their schedules so filled with people in trouble that they cannot take any more. Yet, millions are desperately seeking help. Here is where the church can be of service by putting into practice the priesthood of believers. Each Christian should be a priest to his neighbor by listening to his tale of woe with understanding and sympathy. Just as we have blood banks to help people in need, so every church in every community ought to be a *love bank*. People in trouble should be able to look at a church and say, "There is where I can get some love and understanding. They will listen to me. They will tell me about love. They will help me." But, frankly, is that the case with the church today? How many people look at this church in terms of a love bank? If this or any church is to be Christian, it must be concerned about the social sores and injustices that exist in our society.

Personal Christianity

To be Christian without being religious has a personal application, too. James says, "and to keep oneself unstained from the world." Christianity is not a social gospel or an individual gospel. It is both. A Christian walks on two legs: the individual and social application of the gospel to life. To be a Christian is to keep unspotted from the world. He must be different from the world. He is called upon to live a clean life in a dirty world. This is quite different from what we have been hearing in recent years. We have been told that we should get out into the world and become a secular Christian. We are to be so much a part of the world that we would be lost in it. But James says that friendship with the world is enmity with God. No, we are not to be of the world even though we are in it. We must be as different from the world as light is from darkness.

The problem is keeping unstained from this world. Is it really possible to live a clean life in a dirty world? We are living in a physical world of pollution and in a mental world of pornography. Can you avoid getting dirty? A group of young people went to visit a coal mine. One girl had on a lovely pure white dress. She was told that she had better change because the dress would get dirty. No, she would not change because she would be careful not to touch the coal. She was careful and did not touch the coal, but when she came out the coal dust in the air turned her white dress to a grey dress. She could not avoid the dirt of the mine. We cannot live in a dirty world without getting dirty with sin.

How then can a person be a Christian in a non-Christian world? We cannot avoid getting stained by sin, but we Christians have a way of getting clean. It calls for a daily washing of the soul. Here is where we become truly Christian, because we turn to Christ to make us clean from sin. Once Jesus said, "You are clean by the word that I have spoken to you." The New Testament assures us that the blood of Christ cleanses us from all unrighteousness. The Bible assures us that the Holy Spirit can flush out all the ugliness and dirt in our souls. There is the washing of regeneration by the Spirit that comes in and through the Word of God. For this reason, a Christian is ever confessing his sins, repenting daily, and coming to Christ to be washed that he might be clean and refreshed.

In the movie, *Oh God!*, George Burns plays the part of God and John Denver is the manager of a supermarket. God appears to Denver who protests that he is not a religious person. God replies that he has nothing to do with religion, only faith. Indeed, God hates our religiosity which is a sham for the real thing. The world has enough religion; it needs more true Christianity. God has more than enough religion; he wants true faith which is expressed in deeds of love. Does it make you wonder: am I a religious or a Christian person?

Favoritism Forbidden

The Sixteenth Sunday After Pentecost

Barbara Brokhoff

My brothers, as believers in our glorious Lord Jesus Christ, don't show favoritism. [James 2:1]

There is a common adage in our world which says, "It's not so much *what* you know, it's *who* you know!"

James, in the words of this text, is reminding us, in no uncertain terms, that snobbishness, showing distinction of persons, contempt, and discrimination are all instances of worldliness and are completely incompatible with our faith in our glorious Lord Jesus Christ. We must learn to estimate people, not on a superficial basis, but to value them because of their fundamental worth and humanity. God's estimate of worth is not upon the "face" that we show to others, but on the heart.

Look at the way —

We all make distinctions.

In all of society, in and out of church, we are guilty of discrimination, of playing games with favorite persons; the ones who are richest, wisest, most important, and most likely to help us play our games of self-advancement.

So we fawn over people, hoping that our notice of them will make them notice us and then we can take one more move up in a profitable direction. Every corporation has its room where the "big shot" sits. We arrange our academic processions to suit seniority and superiority. We carefully arrange a "speaker's table" for the very important guests. The choir sits at front and center. The soloist is always visible. The center chair, the big one, the high-backed, cushioned one, is for the chief minister — maybe it is even a "chair for the Bishop only!" Isn't it paradoxical that while we make such an issue of proper seating, it is in fact "standing" that most concerns us?

Of course we must quickly admit that there are good ways and bad ways of making distinctions. Who could fault our giving proper recognition to those whom we honor on Mother's Day, or Father's Day, or at a Retirement Dinner? There is a respect for a high office that common courtesy demands that we offer. Because of the fine accomplishments of some people, it is altogether fitting and proper that they be shown our respect and appreciation. There is a reverence for age that indicates we appreciate the value of a life lived with dignity and worth. Such favoritism is good — long may it live!

But James is speaking of the ugly favoritism that showers special favors upon persons because we can be advantaged by it. Such partiality is biased and unworthy of the believer in Christ. The exclusive attitude that only recognizes "important" people, or "rich" people, is condemned. William Barclay quotes a few lines to show this spirit of discrimination at work in us:

> *We are God's chosen few,*
> *All others will be damned.*
> *There is no room in heaven for you,*
> *We can't have heaven crammed.*

To discriminate between persons because of their social or financial status is to pass judgments from *evil motives*. The faith of Jesus Christ does not allow for distinctions based upon birth, race, property, personality, sex, or anything else!

Jonah was a religious snob. God told him to go and preach to the people of Nineveh — "repent or perish." But Jonah refused to go because he didn't *like* the

Ninevites, he didn't *want* them to repent and be saved from destruction. In Jonah's mind they were pagans, enemies, unworthy of God's mercy and forgiveness. You remember he did finally go to Nineveh, by way of a ticket to Tarshish and a time in the belly of the whale, but as soon as he got there and preached they *did* repent and then he sulked because he didn't want God to love them and spare them. Talk about discrimination of persons!

We are equally as adept at making distinctions. The possibilities are boundless:

Education — "He doesn't have an 'earned' degree, you know" — or "She didn't attend the 'best' college."

Ancestry — "She didn't come from a 'proper' background" — "It's a wonder he amounts to anything, his family background is doubtful, you know."

Intellect — "Some people can't help it if they are not as naturally bright and quick as others — a little slow, you know."

Sins — "She's changed, of course, but you *do* know what she used to be, don't you?"

James doesn't mince words, he comes right out and tells us plainly that this kind of thinking is *sinful!*

Someone recently told of a church that had difficulty getting any evangelism done because it had a reputation for being a "gown and town church" — indicating that only the academic and business community was worthy of being a member. Others would not be welcome. Such favoritism of persons comes under the wrath and judgment of God!

This pitiful partiality of persons produces prejudices among us. A little fellow was asked by his mother if his new playmate, Billy, was a Negro. "What does that mean?" the boy asked. "Well, my neighbor tells me you were playing with a little colored boy. Is it true that Billy's skin is black?" The boy thought a moment and said, "I don't know, Mama, but I'll look tomorrow." Wouldn't it be nice if we simply took no notice of the distinctions that we are capable of making of others —

difference in color of skin, in education, in prestige, in age?

Look at —

The causes of condescension.

What causes our unchristian snobbery and favoritism?

Most distinctions are made because of a *lack of love.* To reserve special attention for those who can further our own ambitions is to reveal the shallow and self-seeking nature of our relationships with others. J. B. Phillips reminds us in his translation that "Love does not pursue selfish advantage." Check yourself the next time you pay special attention to the pastor of the *big* church and ignore the pastor who serves a circuit of small churches. Ask yourself if you would pay more honor to the Bishop than to the town drunk if he came to church. (Out of respect you might recognize the Bishop, but what about your *motives*?)

In a recent revival I was taken out to eat for most of my meals. We ate in the homes of various church members. I could not help noticing that everyone with whom I ate was an "Important Person." I was given a preparatory "run-down" on each person before we arrived at the house — pedigree, position, and status were given as "vital" information. We ate with "The Chairman of the Pastor-Parish Relations Committee," "The Leading Attorney of the City," The Prominent Doctor in Town," "The Wealthiest Man in the County," "The Chairman of the Official Board," etc. I could not help wondering why we didn't eat with the "Faithful," the "Sinner-in-Residence," or the "Weakest in Faith." Should not persons be measured by moral, Christian, spiritual worth more than by prestige, profit, or power? It is pride that makes us want to be associated with the greatest.

A recent article in the daily paper noted that many

persons of wealth, who have little else to distinguish them, actually pay to have gathered around them those who are famous in some particular field: design, glamor, the arts, or the theater. They live by association in the "reflected glory or glamor" — vicariously claiming it as their own.

Thus, linked with our *lack of love* as a reason for playing favorites, is our *pride*.

The story is told of one man who had earned a perfect-attendance pin each year for attending Sunday School. He had attended so many years that his awards, when all put together, reached to the floor. He has to miss Sunday School for the first time in many, many years because he broke his leg when he tripped over his string of pins! Our pride is visible in our frantic desire to serve and elevate self.

It is easy to be snobbish. Even when we haven't anything to brag about we can still be proud. Three men were walking their dogs: Two of the dogs were fashionable, pure-bred, French poodles, while the third was a non-descript mutt of a variety of bloodlines. One of the poodle owners said to the other poodle owner, "My dog's name is Fifi, F-i-f-i. What is your dog's name?" The other responded by saying, "My dog's name is Mimi, M-i-m-i." Then, condescedingly they turned to the owner of the mutt and asked, "What is your dog's name?" He replied with pride, "My dog's name is Fido, P-h-i-d-o-u-x!" You can be proud about almost *anything* if you want to be.

Spiritual pride and snobbery is what almost kept Peter from going to the house of Cornelius with the gospel of Christ. He thought the message was for "Jews only." Cornelius was a Gentile, a Roman. True he was reverent and religious — but still a Roman! Remember the vision of the mixture of animals in the sheet which God sent to Peter? God said to Peter, "Kill and eat!" Peter's reaction was of spiritual snobbery and pride, "Oh, no, not I — I'm a *good Jew!*" God had to verbally reprimand Peter before he realized that God is no respecter of persons — and God doesn't want us to be either!

Spiritual snobbery and discrimination is despised by God. Your "brand name" does not make you superior in the family of God. Christ weeps over our games of favoritism, and hangs on a cross dying for a whole world without partiality!

Look at —

The way to avoid favoritism.

Jesus is our best example in avoiding favoritism, and in accepting all persons regardless of station.

Jairus, an important ruler of the synagogue, came to Jesus and asked him to come to his house to heal his daughter who was at the point of death. Jesus responded immediately to the request, but on the way to the home of Jairus was stopped by an insignificant woman who also needed healing. He took time to heal a "nobody" before proceding to the house of a "somebody."

Remember, the church's Lord was born in a stable, died penniless, and mingled with the poverty-stricken peasants and society's outcasts far more than with the wealthy and powerful. That's the way he was; he ate with publicans and sinners. He called a tax-collector and a fisherman to follow him, and he called us to remember that "Blessed are the poor for they shall be called the children of God."

We shall be saved from partiality, from favoritism, from spiritual pride by knowing how head-over-heels in debt we are to God for what he has done for us. We shall also be acutely conscious of how sinful we are. As soon as we see our unworthiness and Christ's acceptance of us anyway, we shall see that we are *all* sinners in need of God's grace — then, and only then, will we be able to accept persons without respect of station.

When Daniel Webster, the great statesman, was in

Washington, he went to a small church outside the city. Some of his colleagues protested that the little church was beneath his station in life. He was asked why he went there rather than to one of the fashionable churches in Washington. He explained that when he went to church in Washington he was treated as an important statesman, but in the country they preached to him as a sinner.

We'll be able to avoid favoritism when it finally dawns upon us that there is no label on the blood of Christ — whether you are rich or poor, educated or uneducated, male or female, black or white or polka-dotted — that blood is "For Sinners Only!"

You see —

We are all in the same boat!

When you look beyond externals, we are all the same underneath. There was a plane wreck, with only a few survivors. Those people on that plane had come from all degrees and positions in life — some rich, poor, young, old, black, white, businessmen, retirees, and so on — but they found a common mutuality in their need for survival. Haven't you been in a hospital with a sick loved one — and met another person, and then been able to completely forget their credentials (or lack of them), in the commonality of your concern over the sick loved one?

We are all members of the body of Christ. James said that in worship we must forget the things that would make us set one another on pedestals and ignore others — for we are all one in Christ. Whether we sit in high or low seats — regardless of our "standing" — we all kneel as one before the sinless Christ — all of us unworthy sinners in need of his grace!

Faith Alive!

The Seventeenth Sunday After Pentecost

John R. Brokhoff

What does it profit, my brethren, if a man says he has faith but has not works? Can his faith save him? If a brother or sister is ill-clad and in lack of daily food, and one of you says to them, "Go in peace, be warmed and filled," without giving them the things needed for the body, what does it profit? So faith by itself, if it has no works, is dead. But some one will say, "You have faith and I have works". Show me your faith apart from your works, and I by my works will show you my faith. [James 2:14-18]

A bishop and a friend took a walk in the country. On their way back the friend urged the bishop to hurry lest they miss their train. The bishop looked at his watch and said, "Oh, we have plenty of time." "But, is your watch reliable?" asked the friend. "I have complete faith in it," replied the bishop. When they arrived at the station, they learned that the train had left several minutes earlier. "Ah," commented the friend as he pointed to the bishop's watch, "What is faith without good works?"

James asks the same question in our text. He claims that faith without works is dead but faith with works is alive. We do not want to misunderstand James, as Luther did, by claiming that James is against faith for salvation. James is saying that faith is necessary for getting right with God but that good works are proof that faith is real. This position corresponds with the rest of the New Testament. In the Sermon on the Mount Jesus taught, "Not every one who says to me, 'Lord, Lord,' shall enter the kingdom of heaven but he who does the will of my Father . . ." In 1 Corinthians Paul says, "If I have all faith, so as to remove mountains, but have not love, I am nothing." In his first letter, John also agrees, "If any one has the world's goods and sees his brother in need, yet closes his heart against him, how does God's love abide in him?"

We confront a major problem in church and world today. Our faith and our works do not match. We seem to have much faith and little practice. How can we get our performance to match our profession of faith? Each of us needs to face up to the question, Is your faith dead or alive?

A Dead Faith

Do you, by any chance have a dead faith? According to James, this is a possibility. In our text he says, "So faith by itself, if it has no works, is dead." There is evidence that in our country we have a terrific amount of faith. According to a recent poll, ninety-five percent of the American people claim they believe in God. Seventy-one percent or 131,000,000 Americans are members of a church. Forty percent of them worship regularly and they bring with them financial support totalling $5.6 billion. How much of this is superficial faith? One man said, "I believe in God, but I am not nuts about him." A woman explained to her pastor, "My husband believes in God . . . only he is not interested in him."

Do our lives match the faith we claim? If we have this much faith, how is it that evil seems to flourish in our society? Since 1960 serious crimes have tripled. America can boast of having the highest rate of murder in the industrial world. Our jails are so overcrowded that our courts hesitate to sentence people to prison. Gambling is the biggest and fastest growing business in the country with two-thirds of the American people gambling and spending $75 billion per year on it. How can we claim to believe in God when our children are raising havoc in our schools? Vandalism costs $500 million annually. Seventy thousand teachers are attacked by students each year. In one year one hundred students were murdered inside the walls of the public schools.

Of all places you ought to find a matching of faith and

works in the church. Do we? How do we reconcile faith with racism in the church? A black man got religion and he considered joining a prominent church in town. He went to see the pastor of the church and told him about his conversion. He asked about the possibility of joining his church. The pastor advised, "Sam, I think you ought to pray earnestly about this for a while." After some months they met again. The preacher asked Sam how his praying about church membership was coming along. The black man replied, "Well, I prayed, and the Lord told me that he had been trying to join your church for years and had not been able. So, there's not much use of my trying to get into your church."

How do you reconcile faith in Christ and disharmony in the church? Many congregations are plagued with malicious gossip, cliques, and factions warring against each other. Some churches are split right down the middle and members of both parties often do not talk to each other. How can you reconcile faith with a denomination that splits for the first time in 1978 after being united since 1789 over the issue of ordaining women? How can you explain a church's refusal to participate in a common hymnal because the conservatives find fault with the theology of "Amazing Grace"?

Is faith dead or alive when only forty percent of a church's membership comes out on a Sunday morning to worship God? Is there much faith in a church in which twenty percent of the membership does eighty percent of the work? Is faith real in a church when less than ten percent bother to witness to an unbeliever? James has a point, don't you think?

A False Faith

Well, what difference does it make if your faith is dead? In our text James says that a dead faith (a faith without works) does you personally no good. "What does it profit, my brethren, if a man says he has faith but has not works? Can his faith save him?" When I was a child in Pennsylvania, we used to call the Halloween masks "false faces." A false faith is a false face we give to the world. To say we have faith when we do not have works is only fooling ourselves and we deceive the world. Faith without works is a sham and a mockery. We are kidding ourselves that we have saving faith, and it amounts to a false security with God.

How can you say that you believe in God and you do not identify with his cause in the world, the church? That is exactly what approximately forty percent of the American people are doing. How can you say that you have faith in Christ and you refuse to join the church which is his body? That claimed faith is no faith at all because there is no evidence that faith exists. If you have faith, you cannot possibly hide it or keep it inactive. It is like a burning coal in your pocket. Just try to do nothing with a red-hot coal in your pocket! Faith not only believes in and trusts in God but also receives the mercy of God. Through faith we have become children of God. We have accepted the mercy of God in Christ who died for our sins. If this is a real experience for us, we are overwhelmed with gratitude for God's goodness toward us. Out of gratitude we want to do something for him. His love causes us to love in return, and if we truly love him, we will gladly do what he commands.

The final proof of faith is obedience. Now we do good deeds not to gain favor with God, for we already have it. We do good deeds because we have been saved by faith, and our deeds express our faith. Listen to Luther's description of faith: "What a living, creative, powerful thing faith is! It cannot do other than good at all times. It never waits to ask whether there is some good work to do; rather, before the question is raised, it has done the deed, and keeps on doing it. Faith is a living and unshakeable confidence, a belief in the grace of God so assured that a man would die a thousand deaths for its sake . . . It is impossible, indeed, to separate works from faith, just as it is impossible to separate heat and light from fire."

A false faith does not do you personally any good and it does not help other people either. James brings this truth out when he asks, "If a brother or sister is ill-clad and in lack of daily food, and one of you says to them, 'Go in peace, be warmed and filled,' without giving them the things needed for the body, what does it profit?" Are you really helping a person who is hungry and cold when you say, "God bless you" or "I'll pray that your lot will improve," or "God will take care of you"? Is this not a cop-out? You are passing the buck to God and you are willing to let God provide what you should be giving to the needy.

This does not help but only causes resentment in the needy person. He thinks very little of your faith and still less of your God. The movie *Oliver* takes place in an English orphanage for boys. There was a scene in the dining hall which was bare, austere, clean, and very proper. The boys marched in and out in military style. Meals began with prayers. Only a watered-down soup was served and the boys went away hungry. On the day of the annual board meeting the members ate in an open adjoining room with a table that was overflowing with all kinds of delicious food. The movie camera then focused on an inscription in the dining hall, "God is love." This lack of sharing did not help but hindered the boys to respect the faith of the leaders.

Bob Rowland addresses the church today: *Listen Christian,*

> *I was hungry and you formed a humanities club and discussed my hunger. Thank you.*
> *I was imprisoned and you crept off quietly to your chapel in the cellar and prayed for my release.*
> *I was naked, and in your mind you debated the morality of my appearance.*

*I was sick and you knelt and thanked God for your
health.
I was homeless and you preached to me of the
spiritual shelter of the love of God.
I was lonely and you left me alone to pray for me.
You seem so holy; so close to God. But I'm still very
hungry, and lonely, and cold.
Thank you, thank you, thank you."*

Faith Alive!

Could it be that your faith is alive? Our text says, "I
by my works will show you my faith." The proof of the
pudding is in the eating of it. Your faith is alive because
it is expressed in deeds of love and concern, in acts of
obedience, and in works of compassion. The reason
James can say this is that we act according to our beliefs.
Usually we do something, invest in something, or give to
someone because we believe in the cause or the person.

Take the matter of casting your vote for a candidate.
Why do you vote for one person rather than the other
one? Is it not because you believe in the candidate and
his platform? For the first time in our married lives, my
Barbara and I could not agree when it came to voting for
a president. She voted for the Democratic and I voted for
the Republican candidate. There was no changing her
mind, because she believed in Jimmy Carter as a man of
integrity, just the man the country needed. I felt that
Ford was the better man and I believed that his
conservative policies were what the country demanded
for its welfare. Each did what he/she felt was the right
thing based on firm beliefs.

When a man invests several thousand dollars in a

particular stock, it is because he believes it is a sound stock, that it will grow in the years to come, and will provide some current income. If he believed that the price would sink and his money would be lost, he would never make the investment. If a woman believes that she is in need of a new dress, she takes the time and trouble to get to the store and find the money to buy the dress. If she said, "I don't believe I need a new dress," she would never get the dress. It is a matter of belief.

Why do you think your children should stay in school and some day probably go to college? Is it not because you believe in an education for your children? As soon as the child is born, you begin to put money aside in an educational fund for the day when the child is ready for college. You believe that a child should have an education for a number of reasons, one of them that it is the gateway to a better life.

Do you believe in the church? Do you believe it is sorely needed to make the world a decent place in which to live? You believe the church stands for all that is good and true. You think the church is needed for moral and spiritual development. You believe that the church is of God and is the body of Christ. Because you believe that, you give a tenth of your income for her support. You promote the cause of the church by your presence and prayers. You give your time and talents because you believe it is one of the most worthwhile things on earth. Thus, church attendance and contributions are barometers of a person's faith. If a member never comes, never communes, never contributes, we rightly conclude that faith is dead. If you were to rent a room in your home, whom would you take? How would you determine whether the person was a person safe to have in your home? G. K. Chesterton told of a landlady who put only one question to prospective boarders, "What is your view of the universe?" She did not ask about his personal habits or the kind of company he kept. She asked only what he believed, for character is the fruit of faith.

When we really believe in something or someone, we will never count the cost. We will go to the limit if we have gone the limit in our faith. This calls for possible hardship and sacrifice. In 1977 the prestigious *New York Times* decided that pornographic films were not in the best interests of the public. The paper decided that it would severely restrict ads for this type of film. This meant a loss of $750,000 in advertising revenue. It was a financial sacrifice in the name of good taste and morals. Underneath it was an expression of a deep faith, worth $750,000, in the fact that a paper should provide only news fit to print.

If you believe enough, you will go to the extreme in sacrifice for that in which you believe. During the Viet Nam War, a seventeen-year-old girl stepped out of a crowd of 4,000 anti-war protesters in Saigon, poured gasoline over herself, and set herself afire. Before they could put the fire out, she was dead. She believed so much in the cause that she died for it.

Some men go into the ministry of the church at a great personal sacrifice. One of my former students was an engineer for Honeywell where he was a highly paid worker. He lived in balmy Florida, owned his own home, and lived happily with his wife and four children. Some years later, he resigned his job, sold his house, and uprooted his family to come to seminary to prepare for the ministry. He took a nearby church to earn a very small salary to provide food for the family during the three years of the course. When he graduated, his salary as a pastor was not half of what he formerly earned. Would you say this man did not have good sense? Yes, he had good sense but he also had even more faith. He believed God wanted him in the ministry. He believed that Christ is the only answer to our personal and social problems. He believed that only in service to God and man through the church could he find perfect happiness and fulfillment.

How then can we get an alive faith, a faith that is full

of good works for God and people? It is not a matter of having less faith and more works. It is the other way around. We need more faith than we now have. Our problem is a lack of faith. Our false faith without works is shallow and superficial. There is not enough faith to empower action. We need to face up to the questions: What do we believe in and how deeply do we believe it?

Faith is not man's achievement; it is a gift of God. It just does not happen if I should say, "You know, I need more faith. I think I will believe more." Faith comes from God. You cannot believe in God by your own reason or effort. Paul once said that faith comes by hearing the Word of God. Faith is a gift of the Holy Spirit who comes to us in and through the Word. If you listen receptively to the Word as it is preached, your faith will come. If you contact the Word through a private reading of the Bible, you will receive faith. If you come to the Lord's Supper with humility and penitence, faith will come to you. God blesses us with faith as we faithfully receive the Word and Sacraments.

But faith is not a once-in-a-lifetime experience. You are not given faith and that is it for the rest of your life. Faith can diminish or it can grow. Like love, faith needs to be fed that it may grow ever stronger. That is why it is important to come to worship to receive the spoken or administered Word. That is why you need to read the Bible daily, for your faith's growth! Your faith will grow as you get encouragment in Christian fellowship as you talk, work, and witness together. Your faith will grow as you help others to find faith and to grow in faith. An appropriate prayer for a Christian is the one spoken by a father to Jesus at the base of Mt. Transfiguration, "Lord, I believe; help thou my unbelief." And the more you truly believe, the more good works will follow.

The other day I saw a bumper sticker that said, "Action People Inside." It was promoting the Girl Scouts. Action people inside that car! Could the same be said of a church? When the people are assembled for worship or study, could someone point to the church and say, "Action People Inside?" James says that is what a Christian church should be. Jesus said we should not only be hearers but doers of the word. That is what we should be, that is what we want to be — action people, acting out our faith in service to God and man.

Prayer — Selfish/Selfless?

The Eighteenth Sunday After Pentecost

Barbara Brokhoff

. . . you do not receive because your reasons for asking are wrong. You want these things only to please yourselves. [James 4:3]

Prayer is not playing little conversational games with God. Prayer is hard work and deadly serious business. A woman in a revival reported to me, "I'd like to come to the meeting tonight, but my son is playing football and I can't miss that, so I'm going home and pray for rain. If it rains my son won't play because the game will be postponed, and then I can come to church — but I'm going to wash his football uniform just in case it doesn't work to pray!" Prayer is much more than approaching God as a Divine Santa Claus who jumps to attention the moment we fling some request flippantly in his face.

This matter of prayer is all-important. The church has always recognized it. Prayer is the most talked about and least practiced activity in the church today. We all talk a good "prayer-game," but the doing of it is quite another thing. We have studies on prayer, sermons on prayer, prayer vigils, seminars on prayer, prayer retreats, and prayer meetings — but prayer is still an underused and abused power in our spiritual living.

One thing is basic: Prayer is valid. Prayer is for real. Prayer does change things; both us and situations. *God always hears and answers prayer!* When God answers us he says one of four things concerning our requests: "No," "Yes," "Wait," or "I'm going to surprise you!"

James, in our text, gives us some directions as to why our prayers are not answered.

Let us look at prayer and see —

Selfish Prayer

James says we do not receive because our reasons for asking are wrong. The one fundamental, basic reason why God must say "No" to our prayers is that we ask just to please ourselves, we are praying selfish prayers.

It is sad to realize that we pray only when we want something. Four-year-old Betty slipped into bed without saying her prayers one night. When her mother asked why she was skipping her bedtime prayers, she explained to her mother, "There are some nights when I don't want anything." That childish honesty reminds you of the practice of a lot of us adults.

What we "want," what our consuming passions and desires are, will finally master us. When our desires are ego-centered, so also will our prayers be. This craving for personal desires to be satisfied is what often slams heaven's door in our faces. If we pray simply to get what we want, then God cannot answer us affirmatively, for to do so would simply provide us with more ways of sinning. The true end of prayer is to say to God, "Thy will be done." The prayer of the selfish person is, "*My* desires be satisfied." One of the tragic facts of life is that a selfish person can hardly ever pray aright. We can never pray as we ought until self is removed from center and God is placed there.

An old Swedish couple had been married for forty years. They had never really been happy with each other. They were always finding fault, quarreling, and fighting. Finally Inga said to Sven, "Sven, this thing is not working. We been married for forty years now. We tried everything. We always fighting. Why don't we pray to the good Lord to take one of us home — and then I can go and live with my sister?"

Isn't it remarkable how many of the requests we make of God are for our own purposes? Do you think we really "need" some of the things we bombard heaven for?

There is no need for our business to succeed just to

satisfy our never-ending desires. There is no need for me to prosper so that I can rise to a place in life above my neighbors. There is no need for me (or my children) to make a marriage for mercenary motives. There is no need for me to get promoted so I can flatter my ego. There is no need for me to win a lawsuit in which my claims are questionable. So why am I making these kinds of selfish prayers to God?

Once I knew of a man who never supported the church with his means, never paid his tithes, never gave an offering. Then he got sick and on his sickbed prayed for health. Can you ask God to restore you to health so you can go on robbing him of his tithe?

Can we ask God to heal us so we can go right on giving him second or third place in our lives?

Can we ask God to treat us better than another of his children? Do we think we have "special rights" to "special favors" from him?

When I make requests like these of God — for myself or for those in whom I am particularly interested — I am not asking for the right things. These are prayers no different from what the heathen would pray. They are prompted by ambition, avarice, selfishness, and I have no right to expect God to answer them.

A little boy named Billy said he no longer believed in prayer. When asked for his reason he said, "I tried praying plenty of times. It never works. I asked God for a new baseball glove and I still have to use my brother's old one. I asked God to help our team win the game, and it was a tie. I prayed it wouldn't rain and ruin our picnic, but the weather forecast says we are supposed to have showers. I'm through with praying!"

Solomon asked in his prayer, not for riches, but for wisdom to rule his people well. God was so pleased with Solomon's request and the motives behind it, that he gave him both wisdom and riches, honoring him because of his selflessness.

There are those of us who seem to be on the Lord's

side, but we are really on our own. We are like the sons of Zebedee. When they heard that the Master might be crowned king, they got into a huddle. "This might happen," they reasoned to themselves, "and if it does, what will we get out of it? We better get on the inside track right now." So they asked Jesus, "Grant us to sit, one at your right hand and one at your left, in your glory."

Our prayers are often so selfish that it is a blessing that God does not answer some of them. We will be ashamed of some of today's prayers tomorrow. The longer we pray "for Christ's sake" and "in his Name," the less likely we are to pray unworthily. The false, the less-than-Christian requests we make will slip away from us the nearer we kneel to the Cross of Christ.

Selfless Prayer

Fulton J. Sheen says, "The man who thinks only of himself says only prayers of petition; he who thinks of his neighbor says prayers of intercession; he who thinks only of loving and serving God, says prayers of abandonment to God's Will, and this is the prayer of the saints."

Nothing so purifies our prayers as seeing Christ as he really is. Galileo visited the tomb of St. Anthony, intending to ask for money for himself, health for his children, and old age for his mother. But as he stood there in the inspiration of that Saint's sacrifice, he found himself praying, "I beg you, St. Anthony, to plead with Jesus Christ for me that he should enlighten my mind and let me invent something very great to further human knowledge." Looking up to Christ and his sacrifice at Calvary has a way of purging the selfishness from our prayers and lifting them to intentions far beyond our first low thoughts.

Prayers of intercession are selfless prayers. To pray for those in authority, for teachers, the young, the old, the feeble, the weak, the strong, the sick, the dying — this is good praying. A poor working girl became a Christian. She couldn't do much in the way of work in the church, but she reported, "When I go to bed I take the newspaper with me. I read the birth notices, and pray for the little babies. I read the notices of marriage and pray that those who are just married will be happy. I read the obituary column and pray that the sorrowing will be comforted." There is no way to fathom the lives that were touched and helped by those simple prayers of intercession. When we can serve and help people in no other way; when, like Paul, we are unwillingly separated from family and friends, there is still one big, powerful, marvelous thing we can do — we can pray for them!

Never do we pray so rightly as when we pray intercessory prayers, prayers on another's behalf. This is the highest form of service we can render to God and to our fellow humans. No one needs to stand longing for an opportunity of service so long as the Avenue of Prayer is open.

I can witness that I am a Christian and a minister today because of the intercessory prayers of my mother. She literally travailed for me in prayer until I was born into the Kingdom. I can never get away from the sight of my mother, when, one day as I was returning home from school I happened upon her — kneeling in prayer in the kitchen. She knelt before an old cane-bottomed chair and with tears raining down her cheeks I heard her plead with God, saying, "Oh, God, don't let my little girl be lost. Save Barbara Jean!" and I was never able to forget or to evade those prayers she poured out on my behalf.

The saddest words in the Bible seem to me to come from the Psalmist when he said, "No man cares for my soul." It is a terrifying responsibility laid upon us to pray for the salvation of others. It is true that God will never take from another person his power of choice. A soul can keep right on saying, "No," to God, even into eternity. God gives each of us the freedom of choosing to come to him or the same freedom to refuse him. So when we pray for another we are really engaged in a great spiritual battle — the battle between God and the Devil for the human soul. We pray that it be finally claimed by God and not the Devil, and be ultimately lost. We bring upon it the pressure of the Holy Spirit who woos, beseeches, entreats, entices, and draws that soul in mercy toward God. We bring the power of love to bear upon the reluctant lost one. So we pray and labor and travail, just as a mother brings a natural child to birth, to bring to birth in Christ the soul for whom we intercede. Blessed indeed is that person who has someone interceding on his behalf for his salvation. How sad that some never have anybody to pray for them!

When we say, *"Not my will, but thine be done,"* we are praying selflessly. There are two things that should be included in every Christian prayer: We should always conclude "In Jesus' Name," and should always say, "If it be thy will."

The Catechism of the United Church of Canada says, "Prayer is laying our lives open before God in gratitude and expectancy, casting ourselves on his mercy and love, telling him all the desires of our hearts, listening to his voice, and accepting his way for our lives."

Did you get that — *"accepting* his way for our lives"? When we pray this prayer of submission, we are, in effect, saying, "Father, it may be difficult, it may mean death, it may mean changing me, it may mean a lot of things I cannot understand, nevertheless, not my will, but thine!" This kind of selfless praying reflects that we have finally learned that *"God can be trusted!"* and that's one of the best things we can ever learn about God.

Good praying, also, is to say, *"God, be merciful to me, a sinner!"* Now, *there's* a prayer that God can really answer! The Pharisee prayed in the temple, parading his virtues before God. The publican cried for mercy and went home justified! It is not always easy to admit that we are wrong. A seminary student recently reported that in calling to invite people to church he knocked on a door that was answered by a young woman. When asked why she did not attend church, she replied, "Because I never sin!" It is a near tragedy that we are sinners, but it is a far worse tragedy that we are sinners and refuse to admit it.

"God, be merciful to me, a sinner!" I try to pray this seven-word prayer every day of my life. Why? Because I need his mercy so constantly and so desperately!

Love Him More

The reason we do not pray better is that we do not love God enough. We have never learned to give all of ourselves to him. The story is told of an artist in London who spent two years, at the height of his career, painting a picture of Jesus. He did not show anybody the work until it was done. He just painted and prayed. At last, when the painting was finished, he invited one of his closest friends to look at it. He wondered what his friend would think of his conception of the face of Christ. When the curtain was drawn aside, the friend studied the painting for a long time, quietly and seriously. Finally he turned to the artist and said, "You must love Jesus Christ a great deal to be able to paint him like that." The painter responded, "Yes, and when I love him more I'll paint him better."

Some of us, when we learn to love Christ more, will pray better. It boils down to this — the more surrendered to him we are, the higher the quality of our praying. The way we love him governs not only our living, but our asking. We spend time easily with those we love!

What's So Bad About Being Rich?

The Nineteenth Sunday After Pentecost

John R. Brokhoff

Come now, you rich, weep and howl for the miseries that are coming upon you. Your riches have rotted and your garments are moth-eaten. Your gold and silver have rusted, and their rust will be evidence against you and will eat your flesh like fire. You have laid up treasure for the last days. Behold, the wages of the laborers who mowed your fields, which you kept back by fraud, cry out; and the cries of the harvesters have reached the ears of the Lord of hosts. You have lived on the earth in luxury and in pleasure; you have fattened your hearts in a day of slaughter. You have condemned, you have killed the righteous man; he does not resist you. [James 5:1-6]

Is there anyone who does not want to be rich? If there is, you are the exception rather than the rule. Agree? How often we say, "If only I could strike it rich!" Then we have visions of what wealth would mean for us: a home in the city, a winter home facing the ocean, and a summer place located on the top of a high mountain. We can see ourselves driving an especially built car costing $37,000. We could have a yacht for sailing in the Caribbean. There could be a riding stable. Riches bring to mind no more work, no more getting up early and fighting the traffic to the job downtown. There are visions of leisure and luxury! And we express this craving for wealth by gambling with the hope of getting rich quick, by becoming a workaholic, by investing in risky stocks, and pinching every penny. In the light of this text, however, should we want to be rich? James says that being rich is bad, bad, bad! Listen to what he says, "Come now, you rich, weep and howl for the miseries that are coming upon you." This makes us ask how we should feel about being rich or about rich people.

Are You Rich?

First, we must ask about whom we are referring? James is addressing the rich: "you rich." Who are they? Does that leave you out? How many of us consider ourselves to be rich? Even if we are, we would probably disclaim it. It is hardly possible that you are another Paul Getty, a Howard Hughes, a Ford, or a Rockefeller. Yet, we are a wealthy people as a nation. The U.S. Census Bureau reports that in 1977 Americans had more wealth, education, and longevity than at any other time in the history of America. Our government, it seems, will not let us be real poor. We have a social welfare state. The U.S. Commerce Department reports that 27.3% of our gross national product goes for social services, Social Security, pensions, and the like.

Do we realize how rich we are as an American people? Maybe James is really talking to us. When we look at ourselves or compare ourselves with our more wealthy neighbors, we think we are poor folks. We struggle to pay our monthly bills and wonder if we are going to make our debt payments on house, furniture, and cars. We often worry whether there will be enough money on hand to send the kids to college. But compared with the rest of the world, even our poor are rich by comparison, the one-third of our black people with an annual income of less than $4500.

In comparison with the rest of the world, we are truly wealthy. The people in the undeveloped countries have an annual income of $182 while the income in the developed countries is $2107. America is still the richest country in the world. We have seventy percent of the world's gold. In 1950, ninety percent of our homes had only one electric appliance; but in 1976, ninety percent of our homes have a clothes washer, coffee maker, TV set, a toaster, vacuum cleaner, and a radio. There is one auto for every two people in this country — fantastic, right? When we consider the food situation we can see how wealthy we are. It is reported that eighty percent of the world's population goes to bed hungry and that seven die of hunger every minute of the day and night. This condition is worsening because each day there is an increase in population of 205,000 or an annual increase of 75 million. In contrast, Americans have more food than they can eat. Fifty percent of us are overweight. It is claimed that fifty-three percent of those who die meet their death by a cause related to obesity. Literally we are eating ourselves to death! How can we claim we are poor when we spend hundreds of millions of dollars each year on non-essentials such as tobacco, alcohol, drugs, and sports?

When God looks down upon this world with its 147 nations, he sees one nation in particular that is rich, very rich in comparison to the other nations. When James says, "you rich," he must mean you and me. We are materially rich. Would that we might be as rich in the spirit!

What's Bad About Wealth?

How should we feel about our wealth? Should we regret it? Get rid of our money? Is it a sin to be rich? Is there anything bad about having plenty? In our text James seems to think so. He points out the sins of the rich and promises judgment upon the rich for these abuses of their affluence. What are the abuses of wealth that James mentions in the text?

There is greed. We never seem to get enough. Profits are never high enough. Wages must go up each year. Out of greed we take advantage of our help by paying miserable wages. We can get rich off the labors of the oppressed. James put it this way, "Behold, the wages of the laborers who mowed your fields, which you kept back by fraud." This greed is expressed in ever pushing up the prices of goods to make a killing in profit. It is expressed in our strikes — the miners, the farmers, teachers, nurses, telephone workers. Who doesn't strike these days? Will the preachers be next to strike? Is there no end to the rise of wages? Wages go up and then prices go up, and so does inflation. Who wins this game? Moreover, we see this greed expressed in our going in debt. The public and private debt of Americans now totals $2,773 trillion. No, not millions, not billions, but *trillions*! Personal debts alone amount to $186 billion. One out of every two Americans is in debt. We are in debt because we are living beyond our incomes. We cannot wait until we have earned and saved enough to pay cash for what we want. This means that the demand far exceeds the supply. This pushes prices up, up, up. Today it seems everybody wants more; it is an insatiable desire. Economists tell us that this greed is the cause of our inflation. It is a moral, not only an economic problem.

Our greed is threatening to undo us. In *Aesop's Fables* a farmer went to feed his goose and found she had laid a strange egg. It was made of a glowing metal. He took it to a jeweler who sawed it in half and found it was solid gold. The farmer rushed home and gave the goose a private room in his house. Each day the goose laid a golden egg and the farmer became rich. But the more he got, the more he wanted. One day he said, "The goose is lazy — only one egg a day!" He decided to kill the goose and get the other eggs inside her. But when he cut her open, the goose was like other geese — no eggs!

Another evil of riches is the false scale of values rich people sometimes have. James in our text refers to this when he says, "You have lived on earth in luxury and in pleasure." These seem to be the top values for rich people. We, too, dream of being rich some day that we can have leisure and luxury. Our craving for luxury is seen in the use of the word in advertising: we have "luxurious" condominiums, "luxurious" interiors of cars, "luxurious" motel suites, and on and on. It means that we can have our values turned upside down. The things that are least important are put on top of the list. For instance, we pay fabulous prices to those who can provide us entertainment. For one fight we pay Muhammed Ali five million dollars. We pay Johnny Carson three million for making us laugh at the time we should be going to bed. We listen to a news commentator and pay her, Barbara Walters, a million a year to tell us what is going on in the world. There must be something wrong with our values or we would not be paying high salaries for those who do so little for the common good compared with those who render service.

We pay a disc jockey $100,000 a year but we grudgingly pay a preacher about $10,000. We pay a General Motors president a salary of $950,000 but we pay the president of the United States a salary of $200,000. Does this make sense to you? We make people rich by spending money on things that are secondary in life. We have come to believe that life consists of the things that are possessed. We forget that we can own all the gold in the world and yet not have the riches of love, friendship, and peace. Wealth has a tendency to distort our values.

James points out to us another evil of rich people. They are tempted to put material values above human values. James condemns the rich, for "you have killed the righteous man." Does it seem right to you that we Americans can spend one billion dollars to send a spacecraft to inspect the planet, Mars, and yet hunger and poverty abound on the earth? How is it that we Americans can spend $375 per capita on military hardware and give only $6 per capita for the hungry of the world? It is claimed that each year 360,000 die from smoking but we give $60 million for the price support of tobacco. The best we can do to protect lives is to put a warning on a cigarette wrapper.

The wealthy have often such a passion for money that they will ride herd over people, make people their tools for profit, and disregard the health and welfare of people just to make money. How diabolical! In the popular

movie of a few years ago, *Jaws*, there was a plan to close
the beach because of a man-eating shark. The real estate
people succeeded in preventing this because they
wanted people on the beach to see and buy their
properties. As a result, one of the young people was
eaten by the shark. What price, money! In the light of
this, you can understand why James cries out, "Come
now, you rich, weep and howl for the miseries that are
coming upon you."

Rich and Yet Christian

Where does God come into this picture? What does he
have to say about the rich which, as we have seen,
includes you and me? Is there anything right about being
rich? James brings God into the picture when he writes,
"the cries of the harvesters have reached the ears of the
Lord of hosts." How shall we look at this problem from a
theological standpoint? According to James the problem
of the rich has reached the ears of God. How do you think
he feels about the situation?

We need to realize at the very beginning that the rich
are not inherently bad because they are rich. It depends
on how the wealth was acquired and what you do with
the wealth once you have it. Although Jesus condemned
the evils of wealth, he did not exclude rich people from his
ministry. When wealth kept a youth from following him,
he urged him to give his money to the poor and follow
him. On the other hand, Zacchaeus was a rich man who
gave half of his goods to the poor after Jesus visited in
his home. With half of his goods gone, Zacchaeus was still
wealthy, but Jesus did not refuse his following him.
Matthew was another rich tax collector, and Jesus asked
him to be a disciple. One of Jesus' best friends was a rich
man, Joseph of Arimathea, who provided a new tomb for
Jesus. A rich person is not necessarily a bad person
because he has a lot of money. A rich person can be a
Christian in the best standing.

By the same token, a poor person is not inherently a good person just because he happens to be poor. There is no virtue in poverty. In fact, poverty is a curse. Poor people can be bad people. An Atlanta downtown church ministers to the poor of the city by providing five days a week a free lunch. These people have nothing: no work, no family, no friends, no money, no home. Yet, among them there is obscene language, some smoke pot. Many tell lies and their word cannot be trusted. When they get a welfare or Social Security check, they rob each other. Often the money lasts for a day or two until it is exhausted in tobacco, alcohol, or drugs. On the other hand, a poor person can be a genuine, upright citizen.

It can be said that a Christian will earn and save as much as he possibly can. He will use his God-given talents to their fullest in the pursuit of money. He will make the most of his time. He will work hard. What he receives for his efforts, he will consider as a trust from God and will feel responsible to God for what he has and what he does with it.

Why does he do this? He does his best to get money that he may provide the necessities for his family. He is interested in providing for their future needs. By hard work he hopes to keep from becoming dependent on society. He wants to take care of his family's needs without having to seek help from others. He has a sense of self-reliance and independence. Some people are poor because they cannot help it. They may be physically or mentally handicapped. Maybe they never did get a break in life for a good job. It could be that their environment did not allow a person to get much of this world's goods. On the other hand, some poor have only themselves to blame by not applying themselves to work. Laziness and sloth are sins. They may be poor because they have not known how to manage their money. They may spend it for luxuries such as candy, alcohol, tobacco, drugs, TV sets, and a car which is not necessary in many cases. Coupled with hard work there must be wise saving and spending of money for the material security of the family.

Add to this the fact that a Christian will earn and save as much money as he can that he might be able to help others in need. William Barclay, the noted British Bible scholar, tells of a missionary who wrote him for books. The missionary claimed that he had no support and depended on God to provide for his needs. Barclay said he sent the books but he also could not help thinking how one has to work and save as a Christian to help those who disregard this necessity. The world is a better place for the rich people who have been generous with their gifts for good causes. Colleges and seminaries have been built by the large gifts of donors. The recent enlargement of the library at the Candler School of Theology was made possible through a million dollar gift of a devout Christian woman.

Some months ago I was in Thomasville, N.C. for a week of preaching. One of the services was held in the high school auditorium which was the gift of a man in that city. The auditorium was located between the junior and senior high schools for their use. In addition, it was for the use of the entire community. It was one of the most comfortable and best equipped auditoriums I have ever been in. This was the gift of one person who as a Christian accumulated wealth by hard work in his furniture factory. Who can tell of all the good things that have been done by various foundations set up by wealthy people?

This willingness to share and help the less fortunate is not only for the very wealthy. The average person can share his income with others for their good. A simple Scottish workman in a sawmill had the practice of setting aside the first hour of each work day as "the Lord's hour" to work for the orphans he could not shelter, the heathen he could not personally evangelize, and the sick and suffering he could not heal. Once a quarter he brought his accumulated wages to the minister of his church that he might send the money on its way. He believed that money was to be used for others. It was not a bane but a blessing to many people.

Every true Christian is a wealthy person. He may not be wealthy in terms of properties, money, or stocks, but he is wealthy in the spirit. He has received an inheritance of the riches of grace in Christ. The Christian's real wealth is Jesus Christ who, Paul says, became poor so that by his poverty we might become rich. Though we may be poor or rich in material possessions, we can be wealthy in the spirit of Christ. So, in that sense, what's so bad about being rich?

The Giant Steps of Jesus

The Twentieth Sunday After Pentecost

Barbara Brokhoff

"But we see Jesus, who for a little while was made lower than the angels, crowned with glory and honor because of the suffering of death, so that by the grace of God he might taste death for every one.

For it was fitting that he, for whom and by whom all things exist, in bringing many sons to glory, should make the pioneer of their salvation perfect through suffering. For he who sanctifies and those who are sanctified have all one origin. That is why he is not ashamed to call them brethren, saying,

'I will proclaim thy name to my brethren,
in the midst of the congregation I will praise thee.'
And again,
'I will put my trust in him.'
And again,
'Here am I, and the children God has given me.'" [Hebrews 2:9-13]

There was once a woman who belonged to a rather emotional religious group who, in their worship, heard voices, had visions, got rather spectacular guidance, and the experience of unusual, supernatural occurrences was said to be common among them. During the time of singing and verbal praying this woman often raised her head toward heaven, opened her eyes and, with upstretched arms, would moan and cry, "I see Jesus, I see Jesus." It seemed to be her "thing" to do, and each time the group gathered it was not unusual for her to repeat those words a number of times: "I see Jesus, I see Jesus."

One day a rather irreligious practical joker, who was not at all impressed with such displays of emotion, decided to have some fun. He crawled up on the rafters at the front of the church, high above the altar, wore a long beard and a long-haired wig, and robed himself in a white sheet; when she began to say "I see Jesus" he placed himself right over the altar where she would see him when she opened her eyes. She was caught up in her usual experience saying "I see Jesus, I See Jesus" when she actually saw this white-robed figure over the altar and cried out: "Oh, I *do* see Jesus, I *do* see Jesus" — and then ran terrified and screaming out of the church!

I hope you can see Jesus in this text — really see him, no fooling, without benefit of a strange spell, with no gimmicks, but in actuality really see him!

The text lets us see Jesus as

A Baby Boy

"A little lower than angels"

Here is real identification with us — the Infinite becomes an Infant. We showed him what man was like — He showed us what God is like. He who was God became a man, so he could know how it feels to hurt. He felt our pain, he knew humanity's capacity to be sharp and clever, but also to feel at other times slow and dull. He knew how sorrow and grief and love feel — even what it's like to have a "case of nerves." So complete was his identification with us that he can now sympathize with us when we have a toothache, an earache, or a headache. He can commiserate with us when we have no job, no money, or no home.

Almost any thinking, rational individual is awed by the Infinite — God above us. He is so much wiser, more powerful, holier than we — it's enough to make us scared! In the context of this passage we see a great salvation offered to us — and also a terrible threat. "No escape for us if we neglect this great salvation!" — We *want* salvation, but like a child who is fearful of claiming a prize or gift because of the strange and august hand that offers it — so we tremble in coming to claim the gift of life and salvation. Who can possibly approach a holy God?

Then the text seeks to allay our apprehension. We are invited to look at Jesus — to "see him" — and suddenly, looking at him — long and longingly — our

Intimidation of the Infinite is changed to Identification with an Infant. After all, who can be frightened of a baby boy in a cradle? Jesus took two giant steps down to come to us and erase our fears.

He might have come, and still it would have been an awesome condescension as an angel — but even angels, because they are spirit-beings of another world, would be too much for us. We are only human and angels have always been a bit overpowering for us. It was a scary thing when angels came to Sarah and Abraham and told them she would have a child. An angel came to Gideon and he was afraid he would die! An angel came to the young virgin Mary and she had to be reassured out of her terror — and still fell in awe and worshiped and offered herself as handmaiden of the Lord. So if this Jesus-God had taken that one big giant step down to become an angel, it still would not have been enough to dissolve our fears. So he took a second giant step down and became man — and then just to make sure our apprehension is diminished to zero, he begins his manhood by coming as a little child cradled in the straw. He came to us not as God, not as angel, not as a grown man, but as a baby boy. Who can panic over a baby in a cradle? You aren't afraid of it, instead you feel so close, so drawn to it, it awakens tender response in you — *you* must take care of *him*!

God is getting us ready to be able to claim his great salvation after all — especially if it is first offered in the hand of a helpless infant.

So now we come closer, to look, to wonder, to adore — maybe we *do* see Jesus after all! What a lowering of himself, what marvelous condescension — two giant steps down to us!

For the love of a woman, King Edward VIII stepped off the throne of England and laid his crown aside to marry Wally Simpson. But King Edward, who gave up his kingship to become the Duke of Windsor, was already a man, and only a man. Jesus, who was God, became man — just so he could lift us two giant steps toward God!

Because of him we'll have privileges angels will never have. We may be beneath them now; we shall one day be above them. When Redemption's song is sung in heaven, the angels will be silent, for they cannot join the song that redeemed sinners sing in praise to God for this great salvation. In awe they will behold the wonder of a God who became one with man in order that man could be made one with God!

But look again, and see Jesus as

A Broken Body

"Taste death for every one"

Our intimidation of the Divine is further reduced when we see the Baby Boy in the Cradle grow up to become a Broken Body on the Cross.

Beholding the God-Man on a tree dissolves our fears and calls us to weep grateful tears at his cross.

I preached a revival in Chickamauga, Georgia, and while there I visited a woman and her ninety-six-year-old father. She gave me two lovely needlepoint pictures and put them in beautiful antique frames. The work and time that went into that gift made me feel so unworthy and so underserving that I wept when I got in my car.

Gifts of great cost touch us deeply. We love our mother for multitudes of reasons, but one of them is because we appreciate the suffering and pain and travail and labor she endured in giving us birth.

But here is God — who took those two giant steps down toward us — now taking another, a third giant step for us! He is walking up a rocky hill, stumbling beneath the weight of the cross he carries, in a little while he is crucified for you and me. The text says he "tasted death for every one."

He died — that's bad enough — but it is more than just dying he is doing for us. Paul, if tradition is to be trusted, met his death by the executioner's sword — just a flash of steel, and his head was severed from his body.

Paul died, but did not *taste* death. The death was instantaneous. Jesus *tasted* death — the savor of it was in his mouth for a long, long time.

Some people die more easily than others: a sudden heart attack, a quick accident, a shock, and it is over quickly. Others linger days, weeks, months, or even years in dying with cancer, leukemia, or some other slow-acting disease.

But Christ came to earth with the taste of death already in his mouth — its aroma pervading every action of his life. He was born to die.

He gave healing to the dying as he walked among them, knowing that as life came to the cripple's legs, the withered arms, the sightless eyes, the stinking lepers, that he would one day hang on a cross-tree and no Great Physician would make him whole. He tasted death for us all.

The shadow of that cross, and its accompanying death, came like bile in his throat as he worked with the carpenter's tools in that little shop in Nazareth. Each crossed piece of wood hung like a funeral pall over him, reminding him of his death gibbet.

Each tree he saw must have made him wonder: "Is that the one? Will that tree be the bearer of my human body when I taste death for the last time?"

What a giant step this third step was! Here is not a God to make us shudder in terror — but a human like ourselves — suffering, hurting, loving, and finally dying. We feel love for him, and awe, and grief, and humility, even sorrow for our sin — we feel lots of things, but fear is not one of them.

But look again a third time, and see Jesus as

A Big Brother and Father

"He is not ashamed to call them brethren"
"Here am I, and the children God has given me."
Jesus is the only begotten Son of the Father. But

now, through those three giant steps, he finally has some relatives, brothers, children — progeny. Most great founders of religions were married men. Confucius, the sage of ancient China, was married at nineteen. Buddha had a wife and child, though he left both on the day the baby was born — to begin his religious search. Mohammed was a father, and permitted each of his male followers to have as many as four wives. Joseph Smith practiced polygamy and encouraged his adherents to marry several women and have children by them. But Jesus founded no family, was unmarried, produced no children.

But though Jesus had no natural children, ever since that day when he took the third giant step down, and was nailed to a Roman cross, he has been begetting a multitude of spiritual children. From that time forward he has been fathering a colossal family. Calvary is their birthplace. The Offering on that Tree has produced the Offspring!

We are re-born into the family of God. We sing, in the words of the popular gospel song:

> *You may notice we say 'brother' and 'sister' round here,*
> *It's because we're a FAMILY and we all are so dear*

and then it goes on:

> *I'm so glad I belong to the FAMILY of God,*
> *I've been washed in the fountain, cleansed by his blood.*

Think of it! Christ calls us "brothers" — and "children." That means he *likes* to have us belong to him, he claims us as his own! And there goes some more of our fear. Family ties make us feel safe. A woman in North Carolina tells of a time when her father was pastor of a North Carolina Lutheran Church and her mother was the organist. Thunderstorms were frequent in the summer, and the mother was deathly afraid of them. One such storm occurred during an evening worship service, and the electricity failed, plunging the church into total darkness. The entire service came to a halt. When the light came back on the congregation was delighted to see the mother over in the chancel sitting on her husband's lap! Akin to that feeling of safety is the reassurance we feel when we know that Christ owns us. No matter what our past has been, no matter how dirty we were, no matter the disgrace we've brought upon the human family by our sin, he still calls us "brothers" and "children."

This privilege has the responsibility of not disgracing our elder brother, Jesus Christ, and God, our Father. Do you look and act like your brother, Jesus? A number of years ago at a Northfield student conference the West Point delegation was having a special meeting of its own. Someone raised the question, "What is Christianity?" There was a brief period of silence. Then from a dark corner came the answer. "Christianity? Why Christianity is Oscar Westover." May we have heaven's help to so live that those who have never seen Jesus will know what he is like by looking at us.

Our actions should remind our world of this one who, by the new birth, brings us into his family. Dr. Arnold Prater tells of a woman in St. Louis who had her purse snatched. She was eighty years old. She had been a teacher in the St. Louis Elementary Schools all her life, and she loved children deeply. They thought she would retire when she was sixty-five. But not Miss Jennie. She got a room down in the inner city and found a job in a day nursery doing the thing she loved best: loving little children. One night after the school had closed she was walking down the street in the darkness when a young boy knocked her from her feet and grabbed her purse. But in his haste he fell backward into the window of a parked car, shattering the glass. As he fled through the night, those who opened their apartment windows heard her screaming: "Come back! Come back! You're hurt — you're bleeding — I want to help you!" That sounds surprisingly like the big brother who took those giant steps toward us, doesn't it?

So now we say, we *really do see Jesus* — and looking, we see him one more time in this text:

Crowned with Glory and Honor!

"Crowned with glory and honor"

No one deserves a crown more than he! God has given him full authority again. Christ demoted himself, but God promoted him above all angels and principalities and powers! Now we see Jesus *crowned*. It is a *man* at God's side in heaven today. The Incarnation did not end when the thirty-three years of Jesus' earthly life ended. The Incarnation is eternal. Christ took our humanity back into the glory with him. There is a Man in Heaven today. A man who is himself God. He is on the throne and he is our Savior! God has highly exalted him and given him a name above every name. Have you crowned him King of your life? Does he reign supreme on the throne of your heart?

A little boy said to his mother, "The two people I like best in the whole world are Jesus and you — but I like you best." The mother tried to think what to say when the child continued, "But I don't know Jesus very well, yet, but I think when I know him better I'll like him best!" So will you, if you'll look long and lovingly at the three giant steps he took for you, and if you'll crown him Lord of your life, you'll love him more than anyone else in the world!

H-e-r-e's Jesus!

The Twenty-first Sunday After Pentecost

John R. Brokhoff

Therefore, holy brethren, who share in a heavenly call, consider Jesus, the apostle and high priest of our confession. [*Hebrews 3:1*]

On the "Tonight" show, Ed McMahon has a distinctive way of introducing Johnny Carson. After telling the audience who Johnny's guests are that night, he says, "And now — h-e-r-e's Johnny!" He draws out the word "here" as long as possible. Then Johnny comes from behind the curtains. The band is going full blast and the studio audience is giving him a thunderous and prolonged applause.

The author of our text is saying to us, "H-e-r-e's Jesus!" He asks us to "consider Jesus." For many Protestant churches this Sunday is being observed as Reformation Sunday, the birthday of the Protestant Church. It takes us back to the 16th century and the days of Martin Luther who also introduced Jesus anew to his generation. Luther was saying to his nation, "H-e-r-e's Jesus!" Jesus was in the center of Luther's faith and teaching. He put Christ in the place of the Roman Church. He preached that we are saved by faith in Christ and not by doing the works prescribed by the church. Luther was a Christ-saturated man. He said, "Christ is the true treasure, the basis, the foundation, the sum total, to whom all are drawn and under whom all are gathered ... So, he who does not find or receive God in Christ will never find him. He will not find God outside of Christ ..."

Christ Above Us

In this text, Jesus is introduced to us. Jesus presents himself before us. How shall we consider him? How does a Christian look at Jesus? What does Jesus mean to him? For one thing, a Christian considers Jesus to be far above him and above all others who ever lived or ever will live. He is absolutely pre-eminent in every way. As Christians we live under the lordship of Jesus. He is our lord, our boss, master, and manager. He is the king of a Christian's life. There is no one greater than he. He is paramount, foremost, and tops in every respect.

In today's Second Lesson, from which our text is taken, the author of Hebrews considers Jesus to be more faithful and more glorious than Moses who was considered by the Jews as the supreme prophet and leader. If one is greater than Moses, he is the very best. If you ever visit Philadelphia, you will probably notice an unusual downtown skyline. There are no skyscrapers. Years ago the city fathers passed a law that no building should be built higher than the hat of William Penn, founder of the city and state. The city hall is located in the heart of the downtown area. On the top of a high tower is a statue of Penn. When you look at the skyline, you will see that no building is as high as Penn's hat. This is the way it is with a Christian. No other person is as tall as Jesus. He is greater than the greatest. He is greater than a Socrates, a Buddha, a Mahomet, an Alexander, or a Caesar. He is greater than a Washington, a Lincoln, or an Einstein.

For a Christian, then, Jesus is all the world. One time Alfred Lord Tennyson was walking with a friend in his garden. The friend asked him what Jesus meant to him. Without a word, Tennyson stopped to pick a flower. As he showed the flower to his friend, he said, "What the sun is to this flower, Jesus is to my life."

Because of this pre-eminent place of Jesus in our lives, he is the key to our lives. We live by him and we judge the value of all things by him. In our day we have a new movement, Transcendental Meditation. For a fee they will give you a "mantra," a secret name of a Hindu god or goddess. They teach that if you concentrate on and repeat this name over and over twenty minutes each morning and evening, you will get peace and fulfillment. The mantra is supposed to get you union with God. A Christian will not have anything to do with this pagan religion, simply because we do not need a mantra to get in contact with God. We need no name of a pagan god. We have the name of Jesus who is the key to our whole existence.

By the name of Jesus we are saved. The Apostles preached, "There is no other name under heaven given among men by which we must be saved." Jesus is the God-Man who paid the price of our sins on the cross. It was he alone who was raised from the dead for our justification. Our salvation depends on Jesus and we look to him alone to make things right with God.

Jesus is the key to having our prayers heard and answered. Christians pray differently from all other religious people because they pray in the name of Jesus or through Jesus. Jesus taught that no one comes to the Father except by him. He stands at the throne of God interceding for us. He takes our prayers to the Father, and God answers those prayers not on the basis of our merit but on the merits of Jesus.

Christians love differently from all other people. The Golden Rule is common property among various religions. Jews were commanded to love God with one's entire being and to love one's neighbor as oneself. How then is Christian love different? We love as Jesus loved, for he gave a new commandment, "Love one another as I have loved you." We love as Jesus loved — sacrificially. It is an agape love, a love to those who do not deserve any love.

Our assurance of life after death is based upon Jesus. In Jesus we have the answer to the question of Job: "If a man die, will he live again?" No one but Jesus ever died and rose again in a new resurrection body. Confucious died and remained dead. Buddha died and never rose. Mahomet died as all men die and remained in the grave. Jesus said, "I am the resurrection and the life." He has gone on to prepare a place for those who die in him. For life everlasting we depend entirely upon Jesus.

Jesus is the key to our use and understanding of the Bible. He is the heart and center of the Bible and all parts of the Bible are judged by his revelation and teachings. Because of this, we do not accept or obey all parts of the Bible. Not all things in the Bible are of equal importance. Every text is not worthy of being preached. Who or what is the judge? What can we believe and accept in the Bible? The answer is Jesus. We evaluate and interpret the Bible in the light of the full and perfect revelation of Jesus. If anything does not come up to that standard, we are not obligated to follow or accept it.

If Jesus is absolutely supreme in our lives, if there is no one greater, then we surrender to him. There is something in his face that makes us call him "Master." Why be content to accept second or third best? Gladly we yield to Jesus and give him our hearts' devotion. When the famous evangelist, Dwight L. Moody, was visiting Ireland, he was introduced by a friend to a Mr. Bewley who asked about Moody, "Is this young man all O and O?" "What do you mean by O and O?" asked the friend. Came the reply, "Is he out and out for Christ?" From that time Moody's great desire was to be an O and O Christian. As we look at the pre-eminence of Jesus, we have to say,

If Jesus Christ is a man —
 And only a man, — I Say
That of all mankind I cleave to him
 And to him will I cleave alway.

76

If Jesus Christ is a god, —
And the only God, — I swear
I will follow him through heaven and hell,
The earth, the sea, and the air!*

Christ In Us

H-e-r-e's Jesus! Our text asks us to consider Jesus.
We are not only to consider him as one infinitely greater
than we, but as one who lives in us. A true Christian is
one in whom lives Christ and he lives in Christ. Christ is
an inner reality in his life. Jesus told his disciples, "Abide
in me and I in you." Paul described himself as "a man in
Christ." The phrase, "in Christ" was the key to being a
Christian. Paul used the phrase 164 times. He put it this
way, "I live, yet not I, but Christ lives in me." Christ is
the constant companion of a Christian. He is a Christian's
dearest and closest friend. In a hymn we sing "And he
walks with me and he talks with me, and he tells me I am
his own . . ." Is that only pretty poetic language or is that
a reality?

Some time ago when my Barbara and I were on a
preaching mission in Gatlinburg, Tennessee, we walked
down the main street which, for many blocks, consists of
various kinds of souvenir shops. At the time a popular
item was a dog harness and leash which seemed to be
starched. The kids were buying them right and left and
holding the leash to which was attached the harness as
they walked on the sidewalks. When you first saw it, you
wondered where the dog was. Now and then you would
hear a child talk to the dog supposedly in the harness,
"Come on, Fido. Now be a good doggie!" We scratched
our heads and wondered if we were seeing and hearing
things! For us adults, there was no dog in the harness,

**"The Song of a Heathen"* by Richard Watson Gilder, *Christ in the Poetry of Today*, compiled by Martha Foote Crow., The Woman's Press, N.Y., N.Y., 1923.

but for the child the dog was real. Non-Christians do not see Christ, feel his presence, nor do they hear Jesus talk to them, but for a Christian by faith Christ is a reality in our lives. We do walk with him and talk with him throughout each day.

This comes about because we are constantly thinking about him and living with him. The great preacher, Spurgeon, once admitted, "In forty years I have not spent fifteen waking moments without thinking of Jesus." After a while, our whole lives are understood in the light of Christ. St. Augustine was one who so lived constantly in Christ's presence that when he came to write his autobiography, he told his life in terms of a prayer. His famous book, *Confessions*, is a prayer telling God what happened to his life. As time goes on, this living with Jesus makes us one with Christ. We become attached to each other. King David had a number of mighty men. One of them was Eleazer. One day he took his sword in hand and fought all day killing Philistines. By the end of the day, the Bible says "and his hand clove to the sword." After living with Christ, we become inseparable.

Not only do we become inseparable from Christ, but we become like Christ to the point that, as Luther said, we become "little Christs." A Christian becomes a photograph of Christ. Leo Tolstoy described Lincoln as "a Christ in miniature." St. Francis was one who lived so closely to Christ that toward the end of his life he received the stigmata. On his hands and feet, he had the marks of Jesus' wounds from the nails driven in his hands and feet. He was so much like Jesus that even his body took on the marks of the crucified Christ. We can understand this, when we think back to when our children were small. Often they would take a nap on top of the bedspread. When they awakened, you could see the pattern of the spread on the side of their faces because they pressed down so long and so hard on that pattern. So it is with a Christian who lives close to Christ.

The world cannot help seeing Christ in us. In a downtown church in Detroit, there is a small plaque quoting Tagore, "When you took your leave I found God's footprints on my floor." When we leave a room, the office, the classroom, the elevator where we rode, the store where we bought, people will see the footprint of Christ. This is the only Christ the world will ever get to know.

A man was in prison for years. The longer he was there, the meaner he became. One day he got a new cell-mate, a quiet man. The first night the hateful prisoner gobbled down his food, but his partner gave him half of his meal. The mean man continuously harassed the quiet man who never spoke back. Though he was picked on daily, he did not reply in kind. One day the quiet man died. The chaplain, a guard, and the angry prisoner stood over the grave in the prison cemetery. The prisoner turned to the chaplain and said, "He was the only Jesus I ever knew." It is true that the only gospel the world will ever read is not the gospel of Matthew, Mark, Luke, or John, but the gospel according to you and your life.

This living in Christ and Christ's living in us cannot be hidden. The leaders of Jerusalem saw that the apostles were with Jesus in prayer. The record says, "They took knowledge of them that they had been with Jesus." No matter how hard you try, if you felt you ought to try, you cannot help showing the world that Christ lives in you. Years ago a group of prospectors started out in search of gold. They were attacked by Indians who took their horses. As they were making their way back to the town, they stopped by a creek and one of them casually picked up a stone from the creek bed. He called a buddy and together they cracked it open. When they saw it cracked, they knew they had struck gold. They decided they would not tell anyone when they got back to the town to buy food and tools. When they were ready to go back, three hundred followed them. No one told them but a newspaper columnist remarked, "Their beaming faces betrayed the secret."

Christ Before You

H-e-r-e's Jesus! "Consider Jesus" says the author of Hebrews. Consider him, again, as one who goes before you. Consider Jesus as one above you and in you, but also as one who is beyond you. He is the shepherd and we are the sheep. The shepherd walks in front of his flock and the sheep follow. The Master leads and the disciples follow. Jesus becomes a paradigm for the Christian. He is the model, the goal, and the dream of a Christian. He is the one we look up to and try to match in thought, word, and deed.

This is a natural thing to do when we admire and adore a person. We imitate the admired one as far as possible. Shortly after the TV star, Freddie Printz, committed suicide, a young California girl did the same. She left a note saying she wanted to be buried in the same cemetery in order to be as close to Freddie as possible. When Elvis Presley died, the adulation of this singing star was expressed in all kinds of memorabilia: T-shirts, jewelry, records, and statuettes. Visitors to his grave plucked blades of grass to take home with them as souvenirs.

In a far nobler way, a Christian looks to Jesus as the model for his life. The first prayer Kagawa prayed after his conversion was, "God, make me like Christ." We Christians are hero-worshipers. Our hero is Jesus who is everything to us. The height of glory is to be like him in every respect. Years ago when little boys had military men and statesmen as heroes, one little fellow went into a public building where on the ceiling he saw a painting of Theodore Roosevelt on his horse. When he looked up and saw his hero, he took off his cap, held it by his side, and softly said, "I want to be like him!" Isn't that the way most of us feel about Jesus? We see him in all of his loveliness and goodness. The goal of our lives is to be like him.

Jesus goes before us and we want to walk in his footsteps and imitate his example as far as possible. A Christian wants to have a mind like Jesus. Paul says that we should have this mind which was also in Christ Jesus — a mind of humility, the kind of humility that caused Jesus to empty himself of divine glory and take the form of a servant and become obedient unto death, even death on a cross. This is not easy, because our chief sin is pride. Humility is the opposite of pride. It comes when we lose ourselves in Christ, when we sink the ego into the being of Christ. For years the world's heavyweight champion, Mohammed Ali, boasted, "I am the greatest!" His fall came in early 1978 and then he said, "I was the champ, now I'm the tramp." How the mighty has fallen! Pride goes before a fall. A Christian longs to have the mind of humility that he can be like Jesus.

Moreover, Jesus is our model in the kind of a heart we want. He had a heart of love. His love was best expressed when he was on the cross. His heart went out to those who were killing him, for he prayed, "Father, forgive them . . ." His heart of love went out to a repentant criminal by assuring him, "Today, you shall be with me in paradise." While on the cross, Jesus did not forget to take care of his immediate family. Out of love for his mother, he said to John, "Behold, your mother!" How we long to have a heart of love like that! Is it too much to ask of Christians to have the same love, compassion, and forgiveness? In 1977 New York City was terrorized by a young man, David Berkowitz, who was accused of killing six and wounding seven others on lovers' lanes. After he was arrested, David's father expressed his sympathy to the bereaved families saying, "I don't expect you parents to forgive him. That would be too much to ask of you." Is it too much to expect of Christians that they, like Jesus, have hearts of love?

We want to have hands like Jesus. His hands were used in service to others. There were the hands that

were laid on heads of children when he blessed them. He
used his hands to touch blind eyes and to cure dying
lepers. His hand touched the casket of a dead young man
and brought him back to life. His hands took a basin of
water and those same hands washed the feet of disciples
at the Last Supper. Here are these hands of yours and
mine. Look at them. Are they instruments of God's
concern for people who are in need? Are they the hands
that are constantly doing good and serving people?

When Christians go about doing acts of service, they
tell the world they are Christians. This happened some
years ago in the North where it was very cold. A
newspaper boy without shoes and socks was selling
newspapers. To warm his feet, he stood over a grating
below which was a bakery. A pastor's wife came along
and saw how he was shivering in the cold. She asked him
if he did not have shoes and socks. Of course, he replied
that he did not. She then asked him if he would like some.
Indeed, he surely would. She took him to a department
store and supplied him with socks and shoes. Whereupon
he immediately ran out and resumed his sale of papers.
He did not even take time to say "thanks." The pastor's
wife was somewhat disappointed in his ingratitude. As
she was leaving the store, the little fellow came in and
asked, "Lady, I wanna ask you a question. Are you God's
wife?" She was taken aback and began to stutter, "Why
— ah — no, but I am one of his children." Then he said,
"Well, I knowed you must be some kin of his." In this the
world will know we are Christians by the love we share
in practical deeds of kindness through hands that become
the hands of Christ.

If we consider Jesus as the one above us, in us, and
ahead of us, we will have Christ-oriented lives. We will
be Christ-centered and saturated. That is what it means
to be a Christian — a Christ-man or -woman or -child. To
be such demands a personal relationship with Christ.
When we were baptized, that relationship was initiated.
But today, what is the state of that relationship? Is it in

good condition or have you allowed the relationship to become distant, if not non-existent? It is important to establish a relationship with Christ, but it is just as important to maintain that relationship and to grow in it. Did you know that David Livingstone was found dead on his knees in central Africa? He died while he was praying beside his bed. On top of the bed his diary was open. His last entry was, "My Jesus, my Savior, my life, my all, anew I dedicate myself to Thee." Down to our dying day this relationship needs to be renewed. When we consider Jesus, this is the least we can do.

Family Resemblance

The Twenty-Second Sunday After Pentecost

Barbara Brokhoff

Beloved, we are God's children now; it does not yet appear what we shall be, but we know that when he appears we shall be like him, for we shall see him as he is. [1 John 3:2]

When a new baby is born the first thing we do is look it over and try to determine "Who does it look like?" Relatives and friends become experts in detecting resemblances. How often have you heard: "She looks just like her mother," or "He looks just like his dad," or "He's the 'spittin image' of his grandpa," or "He has the McFarland (or whatever) mouth," (or nose, or ears, or hair)? On and on the survey goes.

I talked to a minister's wife recently, a beautiful woman herself, when her lovely seventeen-year-old daughter came up and joined the conversation. The mother introduced her, saying, "This is our daughter, Julie." Julie smiled as I indicated how delighted I was to meet her and said, "Thank you, I look just like my mother!" How refreshing it was to see a teen-ager who wanted to be identified with her mother in family resemblance.

We can't always be sure about some resemblances; others are too evident to be denied. But Christians, who are born into the Kingdom of God by faith, can be sure about some things. We have a:

Lordly Lineage

"Beloved, we are the sons of God *now* . . ."

My father was a Scotch-Irishman, a direct descendant of Lord Bruce of Scotland. He never failed to keep alive in his children his love for his heritage — seldom mentioning to us that along with Lord Bruce on our family tree there were also some renegades, horse thieves, and less desirables. My mother, German-Irish, used to get "put-out" with dad and would say, "Jim, it's that Scotch-Irish blood in you! Just think what you'd be without it?" Dad would quickly respond, "Why, Janie, I'd be ashamed of myself!"

No matter what your ancestry is, every genealogy begins with God. We are all *created* by God. But this text speaks of more than creation. Here God is not just the Source of our being, but our *father*. This does not mean we are all descendants of God. It does mean, however, that when God becomes our spiritual Father through the new birth in Christ that a marvelous thing has happened to us!

"Now!" it says — We haven't always been sons, but we are children *now*!

"Now!" it says — We don't have to wait till death, but it is ours *now*, in the present! The old gospel song of several generations back says:

> *I once was an outcast, stranger on earth,*
> *A sinner by choice, and an alien by birth;*
> *But I've been adopted, my name's written down,*
> *An heir to a mansion, a robe and a crown.*

> *I'm a child of the King, a child of the King,*
> *With Jesus, my Saviour, I'm a child of the King!*

Who is it who is privileged to be a child of the King, a child of God? The Bible says, "As many as received him, to them gave he power to be called the *sons of God*."

A former student of my husband, Bill Cottingham, walked into my husband's office a while back with his beautiful new baby girl in his arms. She was dressed in yellow, she was asleep, a truly beautiful child. The father was trying hard to hide his pride in her, but anybody with half an eye could tell how much he loved her — and he wanted his "professor" to see how great she was. He handed the baby over to my John, saying, "This is our baby girl, and she is *already a Christian!*" She had been baptized when she was two-and-one-half months old, and so now he could proudly claim that she was not only his child by birth, but the Father's child by faith and baptism!

Anything short of being a child of God is to be without a Lordly Lineage. Being born of God is essential to claiming God as Father. Without this experience of grace we are left at loose ends and don't know who or what we are. An eight-year-old wrote an essay on Quakers: "Quakers are very meek, quiet people who never fight or answer back. My father is a Quaker, but my mother is something else!" We are always 'something else' unless we have confessed Jesus Christ as Lord and Savior, and been born into the family of God by receiving him.

But, while we are indeed children of God, there is always within us a:

Latent Likeness

"It does not yet appear what we shall be,"

It is true that we often look and act like anything but sons of God — but we are now becoming what we shall be — we have not yet arrived.

Hazen Werner said, "We do not become saints suddenly, we become what we have been doing for a long time."

There are no short cuts to being all that Christ wants us to be. It takes a while. When James A. Garfield was head of Hiram College, in Ohio, a father asked him if the course of study couldn't be simplified so that his son might be able to "go through by a shorter route." "Certainly," Garfield replied, "but it all depends upon what you want to make of your boy. When God wants to make an oak tree, he takes a 100 years. When he wants

86

to make a squash, he requires only two months."

There is a hidden, undeveloped likeness of God in each of his children, but it does take time for it to reach perfection. It does not happen to any of us overnight. We do not mature into full-grown, well-developed Christians in a moment. For most of us it takes a lifetime. A sign on the wall of a pastor-friend's office reads, "Be patient with me, God isn't finished with me yet."

Think of what possibilities are wrapped up in a newborn infant! Those potentials are for either good or bad.

Who could know that New York's Son of Sam, forty-four caliber killer, would become the murderer of six people that he confessed to be? The daily papers showed pictures of his father weeping over what his son had done. No doubt when he held him in his arms as a tiny, innocent baby, he never dreamed of the monster he would become.

Seven elderly women have been murdered in Columbus, Georgia. The murderer is unknown at this time. But whoever that cruel person is, he was once a sweet, helpless baby over whom some mother watched with hope and confidence that he would amount to something when he became a man. Now he will be a heart-break to his parents and a plague upon society.

But look at other possibilities:

A baby boy was born in a small apartment in a working-class home in Blantyre in Scotland and his mother named him David. How was Mrs. Livingstone to know that in that tiny bundle of humanity was the beginning of the greatest missionary ever to go to Africa — perhaps the greatest missionary of all time?

How little did Susanna Wesley know — in spite of all her fond dreams for them — that two of her sons would change the world for good in the great hymns of her boy, Charles, and in the preaching of her son, John?

Martin Luther's mother — though she loved him dearly — could not in her wildest imaginings have known that she rocked a Reformation in her cradle!

It did not yet "appear" what they would be.

Ian Macpherson tells of the poet, Francis Thompson, meeting an English lady in Paris. He was about to call her by name when she held up her hand and stopped him, saying, "Hush! Don't recognize me! I'm travelling in *embryo!*" She had the wrong word. Of course she meant to say she was traveling "incognito." But aren't we all going through life in embryo? "It does not yet appear what we shall be."

God has not revealed all he can do with us yet; he hasn't told it all. The London *Daily Telegraph* carried a letter sent by an eleven-year-old pupil to his mother. He was on vacation in Switzerland. The letter read: "Dear Mom, Yesterday the instructor took eight of us to the slopes to teach us how to ski. I was not very good at it, so I broke a leg. Thank goodness it was not *my* leg! Love, Billy." Isn't that the way it is with God our Father? Sometimes our knowledge is only partial of what has taken place. We don't know the whole story yet — we don't have the full picture. God transforms us beyond all our dreams. He changes us from sinners to saints, from crooks to honest people, he turns liars into lovers of the truth, and bad spirits into good ones. The Bible pictures for us what God *meant* us to be — but often when we look at ourselves we are tempted to doubt if even God can make anything of the likes of us. But he can! He does! And he will! We will all look better after God is finished with us!

The last resemblance of the Divine-Family promised us in this text is almost too good to be true, almost too much to expect — but it is a promise given, and we may as well claim it — for we shall be:

Like Him at Last!

"But we know that when he appears we shall be like him, for we shall see him as he is."

There is no vague uncertainty in these words — but positive assurance. Other people may see us as very ordinary mortals, and so we are, but we *know* God is working in us. Little by little we are being changed into the very image of Christ.

There is a legend about a hunchback prince. He was so bent and deformed and unattractive — just the opposite of what a prince of royal blood is expected to be: stalwart, tall, strong, manly, and handsome. The prince commissioned a sculptor to fashion a statue of marble, not as he was, but as he desired to be. The statue was completed and placed in the private courtyard of the prince. Every day the prince came and looked at it. He would stretch his shoulders back as far as he could, reaching, and stretching, and willing himself to be the man he saw in marble. Day after day he did this, and finally one day, many years later, the prince became the man in the statue. Those who saw him and the marble figure recognized them as one and the same.

Gradually we are growing into the image of Christ. We try and fail, but we keep looking to him, our great Example. We discipline ourselves, we respond to his grace, and while the image remains distorted, blurred, and imperfect — we still know that when we shall see him we shall be like him — perfect and complete at last! Imagine that! Like Jesus!

Human Becomings

The Twenty-third Sunday After Pentecost

John R. Brokhoff

For good news came to us as to them; but the message which they heard did not benefit them, because it did not meet with faith in the hearers. For we who have believed enter that rest, as he has said, "As I swore in my wrath, they shall never enter my rest," although his works were finished from the foundation of the world. For he has somewhere spoken of the seventh day in this way, "And God rested on the seventh day from all his works." And again in this place, he said, "They shall never enter my rest." Since therefore it remains for some to enter it, and those who formerly received the good news failed to enter because of disobedience, again he sets a certain day, "Today", saying through David so long afterward, in the words already quoted, "Today, when you hear his voice, do not harden your hearts." For if Joshua had given them rest, God would not speak later of another day. So then, there remains a sabbath rest for the people of God; for whoever enters God's rest also ceases from his labors as God did from his. [Hebrews 4:2-10]

Probably the longest walk in American history was an Indian pilgrimage from California to Washington, D.C. in 1978. In February, 180 men, women, and children set out on a six months' walk under the leadership of Chief Eagle Feather, a Sioux holy man. With them they carried a pipe filled with tobacco which was smoked in Washington in July. President Carter was invited to smoke the pipe with them while they gave their criticism of pending anti-Indian legislation before Congress.

According to Hebrews, we have an even longer walk, a pilgrimage through life. It begins the day we were born and will continue until death. We are on the way to the promised land of God's rest. An unknown person once wrote, "I shall pass through this world but once, any good therefore that I can do or any kindness I can show to any human being, let me do it now. Let me not defer or neglect it, for I shall not pass this way again."

In this short Scripture passage the word "rest" is used seven times. What is God's rest? It is not the rest of the body but of the soul. It is not a cessation temporarily of activity as the military's rest and recreation, or the time out in sports, or the intermission of a drama, or the coffee break in business. It is not, also, peace of mind but the peace of God. To enter into God's rest is to have peace, harmony, and oneness with God. It is another word for "salvation." According to the author of Hebrews, Christians are on a pilgrimage of salvation. It is not a once-in-a-lifetime occurrence or experience but a lifelong becoming. Christians are not only human beings; they are human *becomings*. What does all of this mean to you and me? Let us now turn to the text for an explanation.

Enter God's Rest

To begin with, a human becoming must make a start and from that point he becomes. A human becoming enters into God's rest. Hebrews says, "For we who have believed enter that rest." It is not enough to be a human being. As humans we are by nature sinful in thought, word, and deed. Since Adam's fall, we are a deprived and a depraved humanity. We are slaves to selves, selfishness, and sin. We need to get connected with our Creator, to be reconciled, to be born spiritually, and to walk with him in this pilgrimage. This entrance takes place at our baptism when we enter into God's rest and peace. In his grace he adopts us as his children and we become members of his Kingdom. Baptism is a covenant in which God becomes our Father and we become his people.

If we do not enter God's rest, we have no rest. Augustine's famous words come to mind: "Thou hast made us for thyself, and the heart of man is restless until it finds its rest in Thee." That is true with life here and now. A godless person is a restless person. Isaiah confirms this: "The wicked are like the tossing sea; for it cannot rest and its waters toss up mire and dirt. There is no peace, says my God, for the wicked." When we are without God, we get nervous. We shift and turn; we cannot be satisfied with anything. We move here for a while and then we get tired of it and go elsewhere. We seem to be constantly on the go. Without God people have no roots or anchors to hold them steady. At age seventy-one, Greta Garbo was interviewed by a magazine correspondent. She confessed to him, "I'm restless everywhere and can't stay put. I would like to live differently somewhere, if only I knew where I could go." People without God look to various answers to their uneasiness. They try to find peace by fleeing the hassle of everyday life with its problems and demands. Some look for an escape in alcohol. Others try sex. Many today turn to drugs to get out of it all by taking a trip, a high. Film Star Dyan Cannon went through a low period of her life and then found rest in God. She explained, "I found my own peace and I don't have to reach for a cigarette, or a joint, or LSD."

There is no rest for the godless in the next world also. The condition of the godless dead is described as hell. In Jesus' parable of Lazarus and Dives, we get an insight into the misery of one who went to hell. You will remember how he cried out because he was in torment. He longed for a drop of water to cool his misery. Jesus described hell as a place "where their worm does not die, and the fire is not quenched." Hell therefore is a condition of separation from God. Souls are not sharing God's rest. To be without God is a horrible, terrible situation.

Why are people not in God's rest? Has God chosen some for life and others for hell? According to our text, God does not desire any soul to perish or to be excluded from his mercy. God invites, seeks, and begs all human beings to come to him and live. Our text says, "For good news came to us just as to them; but the message which they heard did not benefit them, because it did not meet with faith in the hearers." The gospel was preached to all. Who can possibly be ignorant of the good news of God's love in our day of mass media? The gospel is proclaimed to all people everywhere. It is a call to enter into God's rest. They hear the call but they do not respond because they lack faith. It is not enough to hear the Word proclaimed. It needs to be received in faith.

Preaching is a partnership of both pulpit and pew. The pulpit announces the good news and the pew receives it. If one or the other fails in his part, the communication breaks down. A broadcaster can broadcast twenty-four hours a day the most wonderful news but it is all in vain if the receiver is not turned on. As Jesus taught in the parable of the sower, there are different ways of hearing God's Word. There is an indifferent hearing; we hear it with a "Ho-hum" attitude. We can hear with critical ears and then we look only for errors or disagreements with the message. We can hear with skeptical ears and we will reject the message. Hebrews says that the gospel must be met with faith. This means that a message from God needs to be eagerly received. The mind and heart are anxious to hear what is said.

Then the message needs to be believed. It is easy to hear something but let it go out the other ear. The gospel is to be believed and then acted upon. Believing is doing. When people heard the first sermon on Pentecost, they asked, "What must we do?" The gospel of God's mercy calls for a response in terms of repentance and surrender.

Grow in God's Rest

Now that we have entered God's rest by faith, we need to grow in that rest. It is not enough to be a human being, because we humans are imperfect. Though we are in God's rest, we are coming into a full possession of that rest. In our text we get the emphasis upon the present becoming: "Today, when you hear his voice, do not harden your hearts." Today is the day to become, to grow, and to improve. It is common knowledge that if anyone stops growing, he dies. You either grow or you die; there is no middle ground. We need to grow because we are imperfect, far from the goal of the total rest in God. Who will deny this? Does anyone have perfect faith? Is anyone's life a paragon of virtue? Can anyone say he is filled to overflowing with the Spirit? Is everyone in a state of total grace? Facts indicate that though we are nominally Christians, we have a long way to go to become what we are. A recent poll in America reports that 95% believe in God, 86% believe they are living a good life, and 66% belong to a church. At the same time we live in a society that faces tremendous problems of violence, racism, ecology, misbehavior, lack of personal integrity, distrust in government, and violence in schools. The gap between profession and practice proves we need to do a lot of becoming in God's rest.

It is "today" in our pilgrimage into God's rest. When we enter God's rest by faith, we are saved, but it also can be said that we are being saved. It is not only an act but a process that continues throughout the pilgrimage. Luther put it this way: "This life, therefore, is not righteousness but growth in righteousness; not health but healing; not being but becoming; not rest but exercise. We are not yet what we shall be, but we are growing toward it. The process is not yet finished, but it is going on. This is not the end, but it is the road. All does not yet gleam in glory, but all is being purified." This life is the today of our pilgrimage. We are people on the way to the promised land of God's rest. It is day after day after day, step by step, mile by mile until the destination is realized.

A human becoming grows into God's rest. How do we grow in our relationship with God? Just as we grow physically and mentally, we grow spiritually. In our house we have a few African violet plants. Several of them have not bloomed for some time. The other day I picked up a book on African violets. It said that to have blooms you had to have the right temperature, not over 70 and not lower than 65 degrees. You should give them the right amount of water, not cold water but room-temperature water. Then there must be just the right amount of sunlight. To bloom they need to be in the sun, but not too much sun. What care we take to get our plants to grow! What trouble we go to in seeing that our children grow up: good food, fresh air, sufficient exercise, medical care, and vitamins. If our souls are to grow, we must give them the same attention and nurture.

Here are some things you can do to nurture your spiritual life. Make it a definite practice of your life to spend some time each day alone with God in personal devotions. Find yourself a place where you can get away from the family and the phone. Be alone with God. Let there be solitude for a time of reflection and meditation. Think about God and yourself in relation to God. There will come to you a deep sense of peace. You will find who you are, what you are here for, and what God wants you to do with your life. This quiet time in an "upper room" will become the most precious period of the day.

You can grow if you feed your soul on reading. The best book, of course, is the Bible. There is no substitute. Read it devotionally, not critically. Remember that it is God's Word and through this Word God will speak to you and your situation. Read a passage and then ask questions about it as they relate to your life. Read Christian literature that will be both educational and inspirational. In addition to the Bible, keep reading a book over a period of time, perhaps a chapter a day.

Worship is an indispensible way to feed your soul. Going to church Sunday after Sunday can become a meaningless habit, but do not allow it to become so. Go to church to grow spiritually. You are going to be with God, to praise him in the company of fellow believers, and to hear his Word proclaimed by his servant. Receive the sacraments in faith. Let yourself get caught up in the spirit of the service and sing your heart out in praise and thanksgiving. Then you will leave the church a stronger person and closer to God.

Association with believers in Christ can fortify your own faith. One little voice seems so frail and weak, but let that little voice of yours join with several hundred other voices and what a difference! As one voice, all say "I believe" or "Our Father" or "I confess unto Thee . . ." The faith and love of God are contagious. Christian fellowship cements and upbuilds faith.

One of the best ways to grow in your relationship with God is service. Get involved in Christ's work whether in or out of the church. A day spent in a hospital carrying flowers to the sick, an hour spent visiting a lonely person in a nursing home, an afternoon spent working for youth as a counselor will develop your relationship with God. You are a human becoming, becoming ever closer to Christ and ever deeper into God's rest.

Complete in God's Rest

We can enter into God's rest and continue in it as we grow day by day, but for how long? The becoming has to have an end, a goal, a destination. Our text says, "So then, there remains a sabbath rest for the people of God." What is that "sabbath rest"? Do we Christians know where we are headed and what our final destination is? We may be in the situation of a forlorn puppy in a packing crate at a railroad depot. It was stranded there because it had chewed off the destination label on its packing crate. Consequently, no one knew where to send the puppy; it lost its destination. If you do not know where you are going, you are lost. The Christian has a final destination for his pilgrimage of faith. It is the promised land of God's rest, to be at home and to be at one with God. Call it heaven, if you will. It is a land of rest in God, a perfect peace.

Just beginning a pilgrimage, just continuing for a time on the pilgrimage will not get you to the destination. To get to the end there must be determination and persistence. Getting close is not close enough. Jesus told a lawyer who had all the right answers to the law that he was not far from the Kingdom. He was close but he was not in it. During the severe winter of 1978, a news story told of a boy who went out of his house during a blizzard. He never came back and his family searched for him for days. One day as the mailman came up to the front door to leave mail, he noticed a shoe sticking out of a high snow bank. It turned out to be the missing son. He was only fifteen feet away from the front door of his home. He almost made it home safely — almost is not enough.

The same is the case with human becomings on the spiritual pilgrimage. There is always the danger that we will drop out before the goal is reached. Our text explains why some do not come to the destination of God's complete rest: "Those who formerly received the good news failed to enter because of disobedience." The author is referring to the Israelites who became disobedient when they murmured against God because they had no water. When they heard the minority report of the spies to enter the land, they refused to go. Because they disobeyed God, they were not allowed to enter the Promised Land.

Our disobedience to God can cause us to fail in entering the promised land of God's rest. In 1977 two million Protestants dropped out of church either by being put on an inactive list or by being removed from the church rolls. This is an average of 5000 every day or 200 every hour. They are removed because of disobedience to God and disloyalty to their solemn oaths of fidelity to God and his church. God has his drop-outs and some of them are famous. Atheist leader Madelyn Murray O'Hair who succeeded in getting Bible reading out of public schools was raised a Presbyterian. Sun Moon, leader of the heretical Unification church, was also at one time a Presbyterian. The famous New York City killer, "Son of Sam," was a former Baptist. Joseph Stalin was raised in the Orthodox church. Karl Marx was raised as a Lutheran in Germany.

Our daily lives prove that many of us are disobedient to God's laws. A prominent social psychologist estimates that the average American now tells 200 lies a day. Ninety-eight million Americans gamble $5.1 billion a year. In 1976 one out of every ten teen-agers became pregnant and five out of ten had sex before age nineteen. A recent study shows that 50% of the students in American colleges participate in academic dishonesty. In the past fifteen years violent crime increased 300%. America has the highest homicide rate among industrialized nations. We are living in a time of moral chaos. Our disobedience must offend the holiness of God and we are subjecting ourselves to the wrath of God. Breaking God's laws, rebelling against his will, and spurning his will result in our exclusion from God's rest in the promised land.

Faithfulness and loyalty constitute the price to enter into God's rest. The Bible says, "Be thou faithful unto death and I will give thee the crown of life." Well might we live what we sing sometimes, "Faith of our fathers, holy faith; we will be true to thee till death." If we are faithful, we will hear the words of the Master, "Well done, thou good and faithful servant. Enter into the joy of thy Lord."

Until we come to that promised land of perfect rest in God, we cannot say ever in this life that we have arrived. Spiritually speaking, we can never say, "I have it made. I have it all sewed up. There is no question about my salvation." I am being saved. I am becoming a Christian. It is a lifelong process. It is a long, long walk with God to

the Promised Land. So with St. Paul you and I can say,
"One thing I do, forgetting what lies behind and
straining forward to what lies ahead, I press on toward
the goal for the prize of the upward call of God in Christ
Jesus." By nature we are human beings; by grace we are
human becomings.

The Priest With Nail-Scarred Hands

The Twenty-Fourth Sunday After Pentecost

Barbara Brokhoff

Therefore he is able to save completely those who come to God through him, because he always lives to intercede for them. [Hebrews 7:25]

Not all Christian churches have priests. We may call our religious leaders bishops, pastors, elders, ministers, and sundry other titles. We all probably know a Roman Catholic priest, the Eastern Orthodox Church has priests, and the Episcopal Church has only recently ordained (after much controversy) women, as well as men, as priests.

The celibate priesthood has given rise to a lot of delightful stories: A Catholic girl once fell desperately in love with a Jewish boy. They had one basic source of conflict; their differences over religion. The girl's mother liked the boy and came up with a great idea. She suggested, "Why don't you teach him about Catholocism and make a convert out of him?" So the girl went to work on him that very evening. She found that her boyfriend had an open mind and that as he learned about it, he became more and more enthusiastic about the Catholic faith on every date. Suddenly, however, just before the wedding, the bridegroom insisted on calling the whole thing off. "What's happened?" said the distracted mother. "I've oversold him," wept the girl. "Now he wants to become a priest!"

Another preacher-priest story deals with the Protestant minister who had dropped in to visit with a Roman Catholic priest in his rectory. The Protestant remarked, "Father, you have such comfortable quarters here — so much better than my parsonage — I envy you." "Yes," replied the priest with a smile. "You ministers have your better halves, and we priests have our better quarters."

But today's text, and its context, takes very seriously this matter of the priesthood of Jesus Christ — it points out its superiority over the priesthood of Melchizedek, of the Levitical priesthood, and of any other priesthood on earth.

We Need a Priest

Hebrews is the only book in the Bible where Christ is shown as our Priest. Some thirty times he is called our Priest, our High Priest, and our Great High Priest.

The Jewish Christians were addressed in this Epistle because they had been urged to leave the new Christian faith and return to Judaism. They were persuaded by way of persecution and argument. One argument was that they were told that Christianity had no priesthood, no sacrifice, and no temple — therefore it was not a religion at all. But the author of Hebrews points out many ways in which the Christian faith is *not* inferior, but rather superior, to what they had left behind. He argues, we Christians *do* have a priest, we have a Great High Priest in Jesus Christ, and he far surpasses the Levitical priest.

He reminds them that Jesus' office is held forever — it is eternal. Levitical priests held office by succession, but Jesus did not die. Therefore, his priesthood is an unchangeable one! That means that to all eternity he will be the Introducer of men to God.

Jesus, he continues, has offered, once for all, the wonderful sacrifice of himself — and this is forever sufficient and enough. The greatest of all the Old Testament sacrifices began with the priest offering a sacrifice for his own sins. Jesus never had to make this sacrifice, for he was without sin. The Levitical high priest was just another sinful man offering an animal sacrifice. Jesus Christ was the sinless Son of God offering himself on the cross for the sins of all mankind. On earth Christ served men; he gave his life for them. In heaven he still lives to make intercession for them before God. He lived and died for us on earth; he is now in heaven to plead our cause. He bears his own precious, atoning blood before the Father in heaven to speak for us.

And then we are told that this High Priest intercedes and prays for us in heaven. Did you ever feel that when you had a certain need you'd like to have a special person pray with or for you? Maybe it was some godly saint you knew, or a pastor, or a Christian friend. You felt they had more "power" with God or greater access to heaven's throne than you. Well, if you felt this way, you were wrong! They had no more access than you do. God hears us when we pray not because of who we are, but because of *whose* we are — he hears and answers prayers for Jesus' sake!

Christ's offering of himself on the Cross opened the way for us to God. No longer do we need a priest or anyone else to plead or pray on our behalf — a human go-between is eliminated. The priest used to go from the Holy Place in the temple into the Holy of Holies, past the veil that hung between them — to offer petitions on behalf of the people. But on the day Christ died, the veil of the temple was torn in two, from top to bottom, indicating that the way is now open for anyone and everyone to come to God! God is no longer hidden from sinful humanity, available only through "chosen" persons, but through the suffering, sorrow, and death of the Cross, God is now revealed and available to all. Direct access to him is ours as we come through our Great High Priest, the One who has nail-scars in his hands! He died once — but he cannot die again — and now ever lives to make intercession for us!

You can choose whether he will be your priest or not. Today we are substituting all kinds of persons and things for Christ our Priest. You can choose to let the high priestess of astrology, Jeanne Dixon, direct your life; you can look to an Indian Guru; or to a heathen diety. The May 29, 1978 issue of *Time* reports that the wealthy King Hussein of Jordan will marry Washington-born Elizabeth (Lisa) Halaby, and that she was raised as a Protestant, but will convert to Islam. Who will be her priest now?

If Jesus is not your High Priest, who will represent you before God?

A Priest Who Is Able

Sometimes we have humans who would help us to the limit of their abilities. My John would do anything in this world for me that he possibly could. But as much as I love him, and as dearly as he loves me, his humanity, his human frailty, might keep him from doing all he wants to do. But Christ is not so limited. We say, "Is anything too hard for the Lord?" — and we answer our own question with, "No! He is able!"

The New Testament Epistles are full of this phrase, *He is able* — in describing Jesus. This book of Hebrews, and other Epistles, say of him: "He is able to sympathize, He is able to succor them that are tempted, He is able to make him stand, He is able to stablish you, He is able to keep you from falling, He is able to make all grace abound toward you, He is able to keep you, He is able to build you up, He is able to do exceedingly abundantly above all that we ask or think, He is able to subdue all things unto himself, He is able to keep that which I commit unto him against that day" — and now here in our text we hear it again — *He is able!*

These are times when we feel weakness, lethargy, apathy, sickness, uselessness, and despair — isn't this a glad note? — It smacks of energy, of power, of exhiliration, of efficiency, of vitality, of adequacy, of abundance of supply — just what we need, whenever we need to meet life — *we* may not be able, but *he* is able!

Do you remember the questions the Master asks in the words of the hymn — "Are Ye Able?" He asks, "Are ye able to be crucified, are ye able to remember, are ye able to believe?" And in the refrain of that song we belt out the answer in reply to the questions of Jesus, "Lord, we are able." But *are* we able? It sounds good when we sing it, but in practice it is quite another thing. In examining ourselves we usually find weakness, procrastination, sinfulness, indifference, helplessness, and defeat — but when we can look beyond ourselves to him we find, *he is able.* So then we realize that we make all our claims not on the basis of our abilities, but on Christ's. Difficulties may come to us, but we'll make it because *he* is able. Temptations may threaten to disarm and wreck us, but *he* is able to cause us to stand. The whole world may be going to the devil, sin may abound on every hand, but *he* is able to bring it to God! Those words sound like a battle cry, they sound like a trumpet note, they sound like deliverance is come, they sound like victory — *He is able, He is able, He is able!* No wonder all our prayers are concluded in the strong name of Jesus, for He is able, he can do it!!

A young Presbyterian minister friend, Steve Crotts, tells of a father who took his eight-year-old son camping in the great Smoky Mountains. Their tent was pitched beside a mountain stream. The father fished while the boy began to build a dam across the stream. "You'll never dam that whole stream," the father gently said. But by the end of the week, the dad began to see that his son just might do it. The young lad lacked only one stone in finishing his project, and his father watched him from a distance upstream as the boy, red-faced, straining, pulling, and tugging, tried to lift the biggest rock yet into place. "What are you doing?" asked the father. "Trying to lift this rock," the boy shot back, irritated. "Have you used all your strength?" continued the father. "Of course I have!" replied the child, exasperated. "Oh, no you haven't, son," said the dad. "You haven't asked your father to help you yet." And with that he went over and helped the child lift the last stone into position.

So with us — when we reach the end of our feeble endurance, when our strength is gone and the job is not half-done, when our resources are depleted — then we have a Great High Priest Who is Able! His love and grace and power have no limit. His supply never runs short — again and again we hear the refreshing, encouraging refrain, *He is able, He is able!*

A Priest Who is Able to Save to the Uttermost

"Able to save completely" — to save to the uttermost, to save perfectly, to save absolutely — that is the best news that fallen humanity has ever heard!

We are all lost, perishing, hopeless sinners. We are in bondage to our iniquities. We are under the wrath and judgment of a holy God (and justly so). And now we hear this word of hope — *He is able to save!*

Sin creates a terrible barrier between us and God. It divides us from the Divine. It separates us from our best selves, and from all that is good and right. Probably the greatest wall ever built was the Great Wall of China. It is some 1,600 miles long, thirty feet high, and thirty-two feet thick. But as long and thick as that wall is — it is nothing compared to the wall that sin builds. Christ comes to tear that wall down — to remove the barrier between us and God and bring us near to him.

Christ's death on the cross cancels our damnation, and his life guarantees our access to the very presence of God. The Christ who took those three giant steps toward us to save us (Christ came not as God, not as an angel, but as a man) — is now that same man, exalted at his Father's right hand, continuing to save us by his intercession and mediation as our Advocate and High Priest. He shared in our humanity, He died to destroy the works of the devil over us, now he ever lives to plead for us.

Christ's perfect salvation includes deliverance from the penalty of sin past, the power of sin present, and is a promise of future forgiveness.

How "uttermost" is this salvation? How complete is it?

One says, "I was a hooker, a stripper, an adultress, and a down-and-out-sinner — but he saved me from that!"

Another says, "I was a leper, cut off from family and friends, living a living death, and dying a despairing soul — and he saved me from that!"

"I was an alcoholic, a detriment to my family, a disgrace to all who love me, and my own worst enemy — and he saved me from that!"

"I was a drug addict, a thief, and everyone else gave up on me — but not Christ. He saw me, rescued me, forgave me — he saved me from all of that!"

"I was pretty good, I was a fine citizen, I was morally good, my friends thought I was 'all right,' but inside me a battle raged. I was tormented by the guilt of my sin and the consciousness of my estrangement from God — but Jesus saved me from that!"

Ask the slave-trader John Newton, ask the "chief of sinners" the Apostle Paul, ask the profligate Augustine, ask *me* — ask us all — and we reply, "I was a sinner and he saved me — *even me!*"

The sins of the rich are not always the same as the sins of the poor, the sins of the Christians may be different from those of the Hindu or Buddhist, but we all need forgiveness and liberation from our sins. In that, there is no difference in any of us! Doubts come to plague every one of us, we wonder if we can ever be forgiven by a sinless God, we wonder if we've crossed the line of no return — maybe we are too old, or too young, or too important, or too unimportant, or too sinful — No! No! No! Our High Priest is able to save *completely*!

Christ can wash you, make you whole, and make you complete in him. A little boy was trying to explain what we do when we attend church. He understood the matter, but he had trouble with the pronunciation. He meant to say, "We go to church to worship," but what he said was, "We go to church to wash up." That is exactly what happens to us when our priest offers his sacrifice of himself for us on the cross. His shed blood washes us, eradicates the stain of our sin.

God cannot turn away the request of his son. He is unable to say "no" to him. I preached a revival, and an old black man, eighty-seven years old, tottered to the chancel rail to ask God to take him — and he did for Jesus' sake!

A little girl said, "How old do you have to be to give your life to Jesus? I'm only ten, but I think I need him now!" So she came to Christ and he saved her!

You can be as mean as the 44-caliber Son of Sam Killer, as important as a wrong Richard Nixon, as old or as young as you care to say, you can be in a palace or a ghetto — Jesus is still able to save you absolutely and completely. No case is too hard for him. No matter how tainted with guilt your conscience may be, no matter how unfit you feel — if you just know you *need* him, and will come, that is enough.

There is never any doubt but that God will hear his son as he pleads for us. He does not need to speak a word, but only to show his scars. Charles Wesley wrote:

> *Five bleeding wounds he bears,*
> *Received on Calvary;*
> *They pour effectual prayers,*
> *They strongly plead for me;*
> *"Forgive him, O forgive," they cry,*
> *"Nor let that ransomed sinner die!"*

An incident comes out of the 1st century Christian era. Two boys lived next door to each other. One said to his father, "You were living when Jesus was alive. You must have seen him often. What was he like?" "No, I never saw him," the father replied. Next door, the boy asked his father the same question. The answer came back. "Yes, I saw Jesus. I ran to him. I felt I *had* to see him. I was a leper." The greater our sense of need, the greater our Savior.

Help From Heaven's High Priest

Human representatives all have their places — but Christ offers what other religions and other religious leaders cannot.

Suppose a man who cannot swim is thrown into a lake. What is the best word Confucius has for the man who is sinking? "Profit by your experience." What is the most helpful message which Buddha has for him? "Struggle." What is the most encouraging teaching of Hinduism for the sinking man? "You may have another opportunity in the next incarnation." What does Mohammed say? "Whether you sink or whether you survive, it is the will of God." But what does Jesus Christ, our Great High Priest say? "Take hold of my hand! I'll save you!"

Ignore all other sounds, all other voices, all other invitations, all other pleadings, all other entreaties, all other beseechings, all other religions, all other religious leaders. There is help and hope for you now, and always, from heaven's High Priest with the Nail-Scarred Hands!

Who is Really King of Your Life?

The Last Sunday After Pentecost

John R. Brokhoff

Grace to you and peace . . . from Jesus Christ the faithful witness, the first-born of the dead, and the ruler of kings on earth . . . to him be glory and dominion for ever and ever. Amen. [Revelation 1:4b, 5a, 6b]

Jesus said that no one can serve two masters. But every one can serve one master. Who or what is that master in your life? Who or what dominates, bosses, manages you in your everyday life? It could be your self, for you could say, "I am the master of my fate, I am the captain of my soul." It could be substance, for money seems to talk to and direct most people in what they do or decide. Maybe it is a spouse, a husband or a wife.

Why are we talking about this subject on this last Sunday of the church year? It is a festival Sunday, Christ the King. Today the life and work of Jesus comes to a climax. For the past fifty-one Sundays we heard all about what Jesus said and did. Now it is our time to respond to the greatest story ever told. What shall we do with Jesus? The Lessons for this day depict Jesus as a king. Revelation claims he is "ruler of kings on earth." Through his sacrifice on the cross the king has created a kingdom of his people. Because he is a king, we are called upon to render to him "glory and dominion for ever and ever." So, we come to a very personal and disturbing question which each of us must face this morning: Who really is the king of your life? Please do not answer according to what you know you ought to say or what we might expect you to say. Deep down in your heart you know who really comes first in your life. Whatever or whoever that is really becomes your god, your king. Let us be absolutely honest with ourselves as we try to find the answer to the question, Who is really king of your life?

The King Am I

In coming to an answer, there are certain options that you have. There are several possibilities dealing with your relationship with Christ as King. One is to say, "The king am I," or "I am the king." Here you admit that you are the center of your existence. Everything revolves around you. It is egocentrism. You are the top value in life and you live for yourself above all others. This is the tenor of our society. It is called Narcissism. The name comes from the young man in Greek mythology who saw himself in a still pond. The longer he looked, the more he liked himself until he fell in love with himself. We are still doing it in terms of our use of mirrors. Look in a mirror and you see yourself. Above the living room mantel there is a large mirror. In the bathroom almost the entire wall is a mirror. In the bedroom is a full-length mirror. Sometimes you will find an entire living room wall covered by a mirror. What woman does not carry a mirror in her purse?

This self-centeredness which makes one's self the king is seen in many areas of modern life. The theme is often heard in commercials. There is the Burger King theology: "Have it your way," not "Have Thine own way, Lord." When a product is advertised and it is admitted that the price is high, the buyer says, "That's all right. I deserve it."

Today's best-selling books promote the philosophy of man's being tops. There are books like *I'm OK — You're OK*, *Your Erroneous Zones*, *Celebrate Yourself*, and *Looking Out for Number 1*. They are saying that we should love ourselves first. We are to pamper ourselves, be good to ourselves, treat ourselves, and believe in ourselves. They call for self-sufficiency as Andre Gide wrote, "Learn to repeat endlessly to your self: 'It all depends on me.' " In *Your Erroneous Zones* we read, "It's your life; do with it what you want." "You can be anything you choose." "First love yourself" and "If you believe in yourself, no activity is beyond your potential."

Another sympton of our self-love and self-centeredness is found even in the church. A top Methodist worship authority recently reported that 81% of Methodist churches do not have a public confession of sins as a part of their Sunday worship service. If we are by nature good and clean, why should we confess sin when we have no sin? No, we want our worship to be a celebration — celebrate how good and wonderful we are. It is demeaning to humanity to fall on your face and cry with the Publican, "God, be merciful to me a sinner."

What is the result of all this? It simply means man has made himself his own king. He has taken the place of God. And what does the Bible have to say about this? Jesus taught that whoever exalts himself will be humbled. It results in pride which is the worst sin we can commit. And pride goes before a fall. The Bible tells us about King Nebuchadnezzar who looked over his great city and said, "You know, I did that, I built it." That night there was a handwriting on the wall which said, "You have been weighed in the scales and been found wanting." In the book of Acts we read about a King Herod who boasted of all his accomplishments before a mass of people. He took all the glory to himself and did not give glory to God. While he was still speaking, God struck him dead. It is time for us to get our priorities straight. God alone is deserving to be the king of our lives. The first commandment is "I am the Lord thy God. Thou shalt have no other gods before me." It is high time that we get off the throne of God and let Christ take his rightful place on the throne of our hearts.

The King and I

In your relationship with Christ as King, there is

another possibility. You can say, "The King and I" . . . This means that you and Christ share the lordship of your life. You allow him to have certain areas and you want to be boss of other spheres of your life. It amounts to being a part-time Christian. You are willing to have Christ boss you in certain areas but there are some pockets you want for yourself.

It is quite possible that a person can be Christian in every area of life except in the area of race. When the race subject comes up, you lose your Christian principles. This accounts for some very good Christians being racists. It explains why John Newton could be the captain of a slave ship and yet write "Amazing Grace." A couple of years ago Barbara and I were on a preaching mission in Mississippi. One day the pastor lamented that he had not been able to dedicate a new piano which was in the chancel. We asked him why he could not dedicate it. He told of the donor who warned him, "The day a black steps into this church for worship, the piano goes out." The donor figured that if the piano were dedicated, he could not remove it. Likewise, in recent weeks we have been hearing much about J. B. Stoner who has been saying some racist things that indicate he is a white supremacist. I, for one, do not know Stoner and he may be a "good" Christian going to church every Sunday, paying his tithes, and living a good clean life. Yet, in this one area of his life, he is not letting Christ be the king.

Consider another possibility for your life. You can be Christian in all areas of your life except the area of sex. There is where you have a blind spot. Last week a minister of a downtown church in Atlanta was telling students about a woman by the name of Moriah coming to his church. He described her as "a stripper, a hooker, and a Christian." Moreover, he said that she was going to organize a branch of "Coyote" in his church, "Coyote" meaning "Call off your old tired ethics." That really boggled my mind. How could one be a Christian and at the same time be a stripper and a prostitute? When it comes to sexual behavior, we seem to put Christ on a cross. For many, living in sin is no sin. Anything is permissible between consenting adults. In 1976, 55% of unmarried women and 85% of unmarried men had sex before age nineteen. Almost two million people are living together without benefit of marriage. According to a survey by *Time* magazine, 52% of those interviewed did not think it was morally wrong for couples to live together without marriage. Even in the church there are instances of the church's ordaining homosexuals and lesbians as clergy. Do you think that all these people are out-and-out pagans? No doubt, most of them are faithful and active members of churches. They are Christians except in this area.

Or, take the matter of money. This is a sore spot for some Christians. It is a subject that we cannot discuss in our homes without a quarrel or in the church without causing offense. When it comes to money, we are touchy. We want no one to tell us what to do with our money. It is expected of Christians that they follow the teaching of the Bible that the minimum gift to God is a tithe or one-tenth of one's income. Compare this with the amount given to the average church — only 1%. This means that most Christians are rejecting the lordship of Christ when it comes to the giving of funds in support of God's work in the world.

What does this say to you this morning? At present, are you describing your relationship with Christ as "The King *and* I?" You allow him certain spheres of your life and you will take charge of the other areas. A true Christian is one who will allow Christ to be King of every area, of every inch, of every nook and corner of his life. Do we mean it when we sing, "Have thine own way, Lord, have thine own way. Hold o'er my being *absolute* sway?" It was said of that great follower of Moses, Caleb, "He wholly followed the Lord" — note the word, "wholly." It is time to surrender all to Christ and let him take over our whole being. One of my favorite hymns ends, "Let my life be all thine own, let me live for thee alone."

The King, Not I

You can say, "The king am I" or you can say, "The King and I." There is still another possibility. You can say, "The King, not I." This is to say that you accept Jesus as the King of your life, all of your life. You acknowledge his right to be your King. You swear allegiance to him as your King. You willingly put yourself under his authority. You would take him down from the cross and ask him to allow you to serve in his Kingdom.

If we will do this, our lives will be transformed. Like a jigsaw puzzle, all the pieces will fall into place. If Christ is King, then all the basic questions about our existence are answered. If Christ is your King, then you will know who you are — a subject of the King. It is said that the great philosopher, Schopenhauer, was once sitting on a park bench. A little girl came up to him and innocently asked, "Who are you?" He replied, "I wish I knew." What philosophers and theologians may not know, a Christian knows when Christ is his King. He is the subject of that King and he belongs to his Kingdom. He may not be much of a subject, but he is a subject. He may not be approved of the King but he is accepted as a subject.

Many years ago there was a farm family living in dire poverty. One Christmas someone sent to them their first mirror. The teenaged boy saw himself for the very first time. He went to his mother and said, "Mom, look how ugly I am. How can you love me when you see how dirty and ugly I am?" She put her arm around him and with tears in her eyes, she replied, "Because you are mine." There is the secret of our worth and dignity as a person. It is not who we are but Whose we are. It is in our relationship with the King. By association with him and being in his Kingdom we get our status and prestige.

If Christ is your King, you are also a servant. This answers the question often asked, "Why am I here?" Yes, why are you here on earth? What is the purpose and the reason for living? Why are you on earth — for any good reason? A Christian with Christ as his King has no problem finding the answer to these questions. If Christ is his King, he exists to serve the King. To serve the King means to obey the King's commands and to do his will. That calls for obedience which is in short supply and unpopular today. The lack of obedience can mean the downfall of a person as it did in the case of General MacArthur. He was one of America's greatest and most brilliant commanders. Yet, he never learned to obey a superior officer, the President of the United States, the commander-in-chief. Because he refused to obey orders, he had to be removed at the end of an illustrious career. As a Christian, you know why you are here on earth. You are to serve the King with obedience. He says, "Love one another." Well then, do it! He says, "Do good to all men." Time to obey! He orders, "Preach the gospel to all the world." You exist to carry out this command.

If Christ is your King, you are a saint. If so, this answers another basic question, "Where am I going?" The King has gone on to prepare a place for you when life on earth is ended. He promises to come again to receive you to himself. There will be a rapture time when King and subject come together. When we die, we will be going to the King. If he comes before we die, he will gather his faithful to himself and take them into eternal bliss, a heaven of perfect love, peace, and joy.

How can we celebrate this festival of Christ the King, if Jesus is not our King? Of the three possibilities we just discussed, do you not agree that it is the last that we should adopt for our lives — saying "The King, not I?"

After her chaplain preached one Sunday on the Second Coming, Queen Victoria said to him, "I wish Jesus would come while I am still living." He asked her why she wanted to be living when he came. She explained, "I want to take off my crown and lay it at his feet." Why don't you take off the crown of your life today and lay it at the feet of Christ the King?